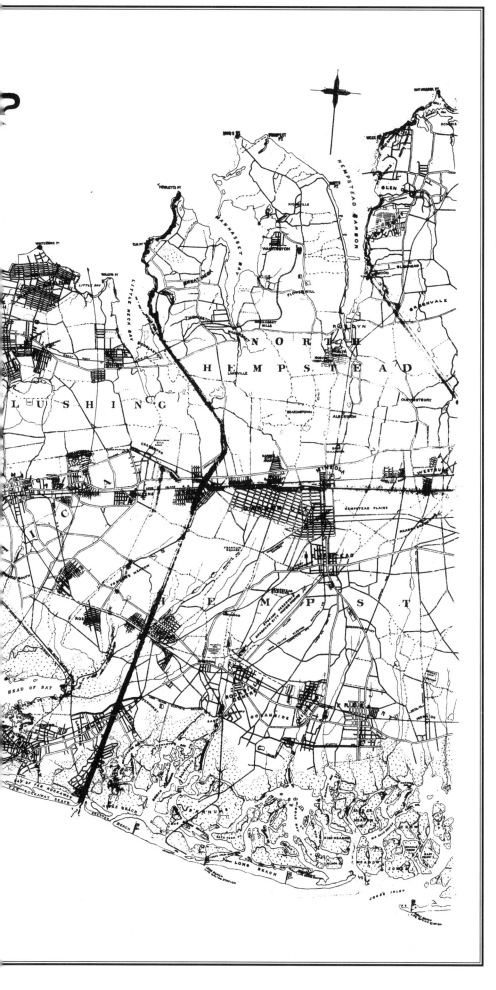

Map of Queens County,
E. Belcher Hyde, 1896.

Lighting the Way

The Centennial History of the Queens Borough Public Library

1896–1996

Dedication of the Central Library on Parsons Boulevard in Jamaica, November 1, 1929.

Lighting the Way

The Centennial History of the
Queens Borough Public Library

1896–1996

LIGHTING THE WAY
Queens Borough
Public Library
1896 • 1996

Published in Commemoration of the
100th Anniversary
of the
Queens Borough Public Library
by the
Queens Library Foundation

Historical Research and Text by
Jeffrey A. Kroessler, Ph.D.

THE
DONNING COMPANY
PUBLISHERS

Dust jacket photograph: Children outside the Ridgewood Branch of
the Queens Borough Public Library, 1911.
Endsheet: Map of Queens County, E. Belcher Hyde, 1896.

The Donning Company/Publishers
184 Business Park Drive, Suite 106
Virginia Beach, Virginia 23462

Steve Mull, General Manager
Debra Y. Quesnel, Project Director
Lisa Arnold, Project Research Coordinator
Betsy Bobbitt, Graphic Designer
Dawn V. Kofroth, Production Manager
Tony Lillis, Director of Marketing
Teri Arnold, Marketing Assistant
Joseph Schnellmann, Hand Tinting

Library of Congress Cataloging-in-Publication data
Kroessler, Jeffrey A.
Lighting the way: the centennial history of the
Queens Borough Public Library, 1896-1996
/historical research, text, and chronology by Jeffrey A. Kroessler.
p.   cm.
"Published in commemoration of the centennial of the
Queens Borough Public Library by the Queens Library Foundation."
Includes bibliographical references and index.
ISBN 0-89865-986-8 (alk. paper)
1. Queens Borough Public Library--History.
2. Public libraries--New York (State)--New York--History--19th century.
3. Public libraries--New York (State)--New York--History--20th century.
I. Queens Library Foundation. II. Title
Z733.Q45K76 1996
027.4747'1--DC21 96-3915
CIP

Printed in the United States of America

The mission of the Queens Borough Public Library is to provide quality services, resources and lifelong learning opportunities in books and a variety of other formats to meet the informational, educational, cultural and recreational needs and interests of its diverse and changing population.

The Library is a forum for all points of view and adheres to the principles of intellectual freedom as expressed in the Library Bill of Rights formulated by the American Library Association.

Approved by the Queens Borough Public Library Board of Trustees
on January 24, 1991.

Richmond Hill Branch, 1955.

Contents

Librarian in Colonial Hall, 1911.

Foreword

The Queens Library Foundation is pleased to present LIGHTING THE WAY to commemorate the centennial of the Queens Borough Public Library. This project was undertaken to help the Queens Library prepare for its next century of service to the people of our great borough.

Proceeds from the sale of this book will be used to create *The Futures Fund*, the Library's first endowment for the purchase of children's library materials. Because of the generosity and far-sightedness of the many sponsors of this project, *The Futures Fund* will guarantee books and other reading materials for Queens' children for their school work and their reading pleasure into the next century.

We hope that you enjoy this book and that it remains for you a keepsake of this historic anniversary.

JOSEPH R. FICALORA
President
Queens Library Foundation

STANLEY E. GORNISH
Executive Director
Queens Library Foundation

December 1996

The South Ozone Park Sub-Branch, 1930.

Introduction

To the People of Queens

This volume chronicles the history of the first 100 years of the Queens Borough Public Library. LIGHTING THE WAY is not only the title of this book but the unifying theme for all aspects of the Library's Centennial celebration. We are proud of the outstanding service the Library has provided to the people of Queens for more than a century, and we pledge to maintain that tradition as we move further into the Information Age of cyberspace and electronic information. Although the ways in which the Library serves the public will continue to change and grow, our mission remains unwavering: to provide the public with equity of access to the broadest range of information resources and educational opportunities that can enrich people's lives.

Poised as we are on both the 100th anniversary of our founding and the threshold of a new millennium, this is naturally a time for taking stock of where we've been and where we're going. We look back with pride over the Library's record of dedicated service to the people of Queens. We note how our collections and programs have evolved over the years to meet the changing needs of our borough's growing and increasingly diverse population.

But in spite of the myriad changes in American life in the last century, and the accelerating pace of change that is sure to mark the next century, the vital role of our Library in the life of its community has remained remarkably constant. Our guiding vision is that the Library represents a fundamental public good in our democracy. It assures the right, the privilege and the ability of individuals to choose and pursue any direction of thought, study or action they wish. We believe deeply in guaranteeing public equity of access to information, which empowers people to take charge of their lives, their governments and their communities. That's what will carry us forward into the next millennium.

Furthermore, the Library, as a repository of knowledge, provides the intellectual capital necessary for us to understand the past and to plan for the future. It also serves as society's collective memory, since history and human experience are best recorded in writing.

And that brings us back to the reason for this book. This volume documents and preserves the story of the Library's leadership as we celebrate a century of service. And the vision and dedication recorded in these pages will continue to set the course for our next 100 years. It's all part of LIGHTING THE WAY.

JOEL A. MIELE, SR., P.E.
President
Board of Trustees
Queens Borough
Public Library

GARY E. STRONG
Director

Queens Borough
Public Library

December 1996

Cataloguing Department, Central Library, January 2, 1940.

Children in front of the Nelson Branch, 1910. Located in Hunters
Point, this was the first branch of the Long Island City Public Library,
which became the Queens Borough Library in 1899.

The History of the Queens Borough Public Library

The Queens Borough Public Library, with a Central Library and 62 branches, and holdings of over nine million books, periodicals, videos and recordings, has the highest circulation of any library system in the nation—and perhaps the world. The people of Queens patronize and support their local branches with great enthusiasm, but this record of success is also a testament to the spirit and dynamism of the institution. Queens Library earned its circulation figures by aggressively bringing books to the public, never waiting for people to walk through the doors on their own. In its early decades, this meant the creation of traveling libraries; today it means providing materials in dozens of languages, offering adult literacy and English-as-a-Second-Language classes, and hosting a wide array of cultural events and self-help programs.

Like its sister institutions, the New York Public Library and the Brooklyn Public Library, Queens Library has always been independently governed, though dependent upon municipal support. That situation has always been both a blessing and a curse. No matter how aggressive the fundraising campaign, no matter how generous the donors, private philanthropy could never maintain systems as large and as heavily used as these. Public funding is the lifeblood of public libraries. The curse, of course, is that libraries are inviting targets during hard times.

During the fiscal crisis of the 1970s, cuts in library services were seen as a strategy of fiscal responsibility—

Woodside Branch, 1955.

with disastrous results. But today, no one would agree with an early 20th Century Brooklyn Assemblyman who derided plans for a grand central library in his borough as "certainly an extravagant proposition and although it may be of use to a hundred or so bookworms, it would never be a paying proposition for the taxpayers at large." It should be obvious to all that the public library is, indeed, a "paying proposition," for above all it is the great equalizer. The library fosters a literate and knowledgeable citizenry, greatly enhancing the city as a place to live and work, and enabling all those with the drive to realize their ambitions.

Story hour at the Far Rockaway Branch, ca. 1935.

Private Libraries, Public Purposes

One of the original counties in the English province of New York, Queens was founded in 1683. It stretched from the East River to Suffolk, encompassing the towns of Newtown, Flushing, Jamaica, Hempstead and Oyster Bay (North Hempstead was formed in 1784). In 1860, New York, the nation's largest metropolis, held over 800,000 people, and Brooklyn more than a quarter million. Queens (defined as the western half of the county, which became part of Greater New York in 1898), was populated by barely 30,000 inhabitants scattered over a rural landscape of prosperous farms, summer retreats, and historic villages. Long Island City, originally part of Newtown, received its charter in 1870; its boundaries extended from Newtown Creek to Astoria. From a few residents in 1850, Long Island City grew to more than 30,000 souls in 1890. The agent of change was the railroad: first the Flushing Railroad in 1854 and then the relocation of the Long Island Rail Road terminus from the foot of Atlantic Avenue in Brooklyn to Hunters Point in 1861 (Brooklyn had objected to the noise, dirt and danger of the trains running down the center of the street, but in 1877 the LIRR began service to a new terminal on Flatbush Avenue). The creation of Greater New York on January 1, 1898, fused Long Island City, Flushing, Newtown, Jamaica and the Rockaways (formerly part of the Town of Hempstead) into the new Borough of Queens.

Catherine of Braganza, Princess of Portugal, was the wife of King Charles II of England in 1683, when the province of New York was organized into counties. Long Island was divided into Kings, Queens and Suffolk. It is commonly believed that Queens was named in Catherine's honor. Sponsored by Friends of Queen Catherine, Inc.

Today the public library has become such a fixture in our lives that it is hard to imagine a time when access to books was a privilege, not a right. We now expect a wide range of services from government at all levels, but in the 19th Century such a concept was far from the thinking of ordinary Americans; even fire protection was left to volunteer companies. Yet, the absence of government in ordinary affairs did not mean that individuals abdicated the responsibilities of public life. Many felt obliged to contribute to the general welfare of their city. Out of this progressive sensibility came the original impulse to found libraries. A second factor was an interest in raising the cultural level of their towns, making available collections of books which few individuals could possibly have acquired privately.

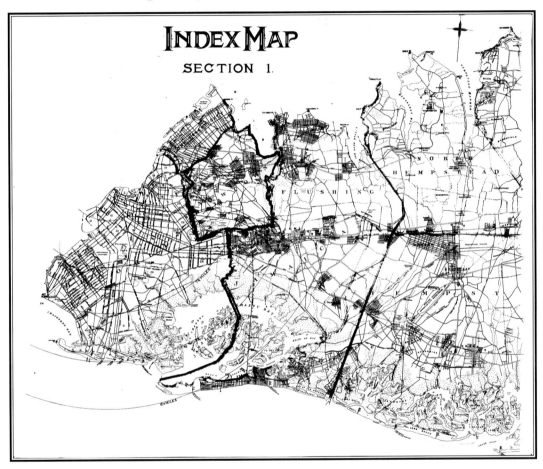

The Flushing Library Association was founded in 1858. Individuals purchased annual subscriptions for the privilege of using the library; members paid $2 a year, or $25 for a lifetime membership. It remained open only to those who could afford the fee until 1884, when the directors announced that "the library shall be free to all reputable residents of the Village of Flushing of the age of 14 years and upwards, subject to such rules and regulations as to such use as the Board of Directors may from time to time prescribe." In 1891 the Flushing Library purchased a small Baptist Church at the intersection of Main Street and Kissena Boulevard, the first of four library buildings on the

Map of Queens County, E. Belcher Hyde, 1896.

site. Two years after the founding of the library in Flushing, leading citizens of Jamaica established the Jamaica Circulating Library; shares of stock in the enterprise sold for $5, with an annual assessment of 50¢ per share. This local enterprise failed to evolve into a public library, however, and a branch of the Queens Library was not established there until 1906.

In the late 1890s independent, privately supported libraries were founded in Hollis, Ozone Park, Queens Village (known just as "Queens" until 1923, when the Long Island Rail Road changed the name of its station to Queens Village) and Richmond Hill. These efforts reflected the civic pride and social responsibility of the good citizens in these places, but those libraries were hardly open to all, and their survival depended upon private generosity. Nor did they benefit from a professional staff, relying instead on volunteers.

Libraries were also founded in the county's factory towns. German immigrant Conrad Poppenhusen utilized the patent of Charles Goodyear to manufacture a new material, hard rubber. In 1854, he relocated his factory from Williamsburgh to College Point. His firm prospered, and in gratitude to his employees he founded the Poppenhusen Institute, a community center with a kindergarten, meeting rooms and ballroom. In 1884, a year after Poppenhusen's death, the Institute established a free library for adults. The Steinways followed a similar pattern, founding their piano company in Manhattan in 1853 and relocating to northern Queens in 1870, the same year Long Island City was incorporated. The neighborhood around the factory steadily grew, and in 1890 William Steinway established a Free Circulating Library and Kindergarten, paying the librarian's salary and donating the books and magazines. In both College Point and Steinway half of the volumes were in German.

Left: The Steinway Free Circulating Library and Kindergarten opened on January 2, 1890; the Steinway family donated the books and magazines, half of them in German, and paid the librarian's salary.

Right: Rules and Regulations of the Long Island City Public Library, 1899.

RULES AND REGULATIONS

OF THE

LONG ISLAND CITY PUBLIC LIBRARY.

ARTICLE 1.   **Hours.**—The Library and Reading Room will be open from 9 A. M. to 9 P. M. daily; on Sundays, 4 to 9 P. M. and on Legal holidays, 9 to 11 A. M.

ARTICLE 2.   **Borrowing of Books.**—All residents of Long Island City above twelve years of age, may take books from the Library for home use, upon signing an obligation to observe all the rules and regulations made for the government and safety of the Library, provided such obligation be endorsed by some responsible resident of the city, not of the immediate family of the applicant, who thereby guarantees the return in good condition of any books lent, and in case of loss, the value of the book lost; or the borrower may deposit as security, a sum not less than three dollars.   Blanks for signature can be obtained on application at the Library.

ARTICLE 3.   **Method of Borrowing Books.**—Every person entitled to take books from the Library will receive from the Librarian a printed card bearing the borrower's number.   This card must always be presented when books are taken or returned, and no book will be delivered without a card.

If a card be lost, immediate notice must be given at the Library, and if not found, a new one will be issued after five days.

ARTICLE 4.   **Restrictions on the Use of Books.**—Each borrower may have two books in use at the same time, provided not more than one of these is a work of fiction.

No book will be exchanged on the day when issued unless for purposes of study.

ARTICLE 5.   **Membership Cards** are not transferable.   No person is permitted to lend his card, or any book belonging to the Library, to any person whatsoever.

ARTICLE 6.   **Time.**—Books may be retained two weeks unless otherwise specified on charging slip, and may be renewed once, either by personal or postal application, provided such application be made at least one day before the expiration of the time.

ARTICLE 7.   **Bespeaking Books.**—A borrower may bespeak a book, and the Librarian will send him written notice of its return to the Library and reserve it for two days from the date of such notice, provided the borrower pay cost of postal notice.

Founding the Queens Borough Public Library

The history of the public library in Queens began in Long Island City. Chartered in 1870, the municipality gradually acquired the urban infrastructure of paved streets and sidewalks, waterworks and sewers, street lighting and new schools, but there was no move to create a public library until the 1890s. This is not a reflection upon the citizenry, for neither New York nor Brooklyn had public libraries, either. The New York Public Library was formed in 1895 with the consolidation of three research institutions—the Astor Library (1848), Lenox Library (1870), and the Tilden Trust (1886); the Brooklyn Public Library was founded in 1897.

In the autumn of 1895, Long Island City resident William Nelson acquired the holdings of three circulating subscription libraries as payment for debts, and he offered the books to any parties who would open a free public library. Galvanized by that challenge, Dr. Walter G. Frey and George E. Clay obtained a charter for the Long Island City Public Library on March 19, 1896. Mayor Horatio Sanford had already allocated $3,000 from municipal funds for this public enterprise. The Library opened the Nelson Branch in Hunters Point on August 3, 1896. Jessie Hume

The Long Island City Public Library opened a branch in Astoria at 112 Fulton Avenue (Main Street) on February 28, 1899, the third branch in the young system, and the first to institute the open shelf system.

was the first librarian and became chief librarian in 1907. She remained with the system until her retirement in 1919.

The Steinway Free Circulating Library became the second branch after William Steinway's death in 1896, and the Astoria Branch opened in a rented storefront on Fulton Avenue in February 1898. All three branches were open seven days a week, from 9 to 9 daily, and 4 to 9 Sundays—a total of 77 hours a week—and holiday mornings from 9 to 11. Long Island City residents over the age of 12 could take out two books at a time, but only one work of fiction, for a period of two weeks.

Left: The revised charter of the Long Island City Public Library, changing the name of the institution to the Queens Borough Library, 1899.

Right: Class visit to a storefront branch, 1917.

The Long Island City Public Library quickly recognized its wider constituency after the creation of Greater New York, and the next month its branches were opened to all residents of the new borough. On December 21, 1899, it was renamed the Queens Borough Library. The private libraries saw merging into a single, larger organization as the surest way to further their original mission. On January 1, 1901, the Ozone Park Free Circulating Library, the Richmond Hill Free Library, the Hollis Public Library, and the Queens [Village] Free Library merged with the Queens Borough Library. In December, trustees of the Flushing Library Association transferred their building on Main Street and about 7,000 volumes to the Library. In 1903, the Poppenhusen Institute's library became the ninth branch. The last of the private collections, the

Library of the Social League of Whitestone, was founded in 1906, and the following year it, too, became a branch.

Communities certainly desired libraries, but accommodating their requests was beyond the capacity of the young system. In 1901, for example, the Tax Payers Association of Rockaway appealed to the Trustees of the Library: "We not only have no library, but practically no advantages of any city librarys [sic], as we are twelve miles from any, with no mode of transit in the evenings." The transition from an independent organization, which grew out of a tradition of philanthropy, to an expanding city-supported public institution did not occur quickly. Indeed, to this point the institution had opened only two new branches—Nelson and Astoria; all the others had been founded by private citizens and handed over to the Queens Library.

The adult reading room of the Carnegie library in Flushing, 1910.

The Carnegie Libraries

The first boost to the fledgling institution came in 1901, when Andrew Carnegie donated $5.2 million to the City of New York for construction of over 60 branches throughout the five boroughs. A resident of the city since 1867, the self-made multi-millionaire had served on the board of the New York Free Circulating Library since 1893. His generosity spurred the merger of that institution with the New York Public Library in 1901, forming the basis for a system of tax-supported branches.

As Carnegie explained in his autobiography, there was a fundamental difference between philanthropy and almsgiving, which, he contended, only worsened the condition of the poor by increasing their dependency and weakening their capacity to meet the challenges of survival. "The main consideration," he wrote, "should be to help those who will help themselves; to provide part of the means by which those who desire to improve may do so; to give those who desire to rise the aids by which they may rise; to assist, but rarely or never to do all." Libraries were thus the most appropriate object of philanthropy, for, as he put it, they gave "nothing for nothing. Youths must acquire knowledge themselves." For the rest of his life Carnegie personally funded public libraries throughout the English-speaking world, ultimately donating $56 million toward the erection of 2,509 buildings.

Above: The children's room in the Carnegie library in College Point, 1910. All of the children are wearing their coats and hats, showing that even these new buildings were not well heated.

The agreement between Carnegie and the city stipulated that each branch "shall be accessible at all reasonable hours and times, free of expense," mandating that reading rooms would "be open and accessible to the public upon every day of the week except Sunday, but including all legal holidays, from at least nine o'clock a.m. to at least

Postcards of the six Carnegie libraries erected in Queens between 1904 and 1906. The Flushing Branch (below left) was replaced in the 1950s, and the Far Rockaway Branch (below right) burned in 1962.

Public Library, Flushing, N. Y.

nine o'clock p.m." About 40 branches were to be erected by the New York Public Library in Manhattan, the Bronx, and Staten Island; the Brooklyn Public Library

Elmhurst Branch.

Carnegie Library, Elmhurst, N. Y.

Public School No. 27 and Carnegie Library, College Point, L. I. 1905

Carnegie library in College Point (Poppenhusen Branch).

would build about 20. At the time, Manhattan had a population of almost 1.9 million, and Brooklyn counted just under 1.2 million inhabitants. By comparison, Queens had only 153,000 residents spread across 117 square miles. Accordingly, the Queens Borough Library received the smallest portion of Carnegie's philanthropy, only $240,000. The original plan was to erect three grand edifices, but the Library decided instead to build eight smaller branches.

Astoria Branch.

Public Library, Astoria, L. I.

Queens Library Trustee Philip Frank explained that "the conditions existing in this borough are radically different from those of the more populous boroughs of the city...the erection of $80,000 buildings would be utterly out of proportion to the surroundings in most parts of the borough... three buildings could not be located as to meet all of the requirements of this section."

Richmond Hill Branch.

Carnegie Library, Richmond Hill, L. I.

17

CARNEGIE LIBRARIES

Branch	Opened	Address	Architects	Total Cost	Cost of Site
Far Rockaway	8/18/04	1637 Central Avenue	Lord & Hewlett	$38,552.96	City Land
Poppenhusen	10/5/04	121-23 14th Avenue	Heins & LaFarge	$30,114.30	Donated
Astoria	11/19/04	14-01 Astoria Blvd.	Tuthill & Higgins	$47,208.09	$11,000
Richmond Hill	7/2/05	Hillside & Lefferts	Tuthill & Higgins	$44,659.20	$12,000
Elmhurst	3/31/06	86-01 Broadway	Lord & Hewlett	$46,246.75	$10,000
Flushing	12/17/06	41-25 Main Street	Lord & Hewlett	$49,980.81	$12,000
Woodhaven	1/7/24	85-41 Forest Parkway	Robert F. Schirmer	$95,000.00	$15,000

Between 1904 and 1906 Carnegie libraries were dedicated in Astoria, Far Rockaway, Flushing, Elmhurst, College Point (Poppenhusen Branch), and Richmond Hill; the last opened in Woodhaven in 1924. The first was in Far Rockaway, where Benjamin Mott had earlier deeded property to New York City for educational purposes; the Board of Estimate turned the site over to the Queens Library in 1902, and the one-story brick, limestone and terra-cotta building opened its doors in August 1904. The smoothest path was in College Point, where 400 spirited citizens quickly subscribed to a fund to purchase a site and immediately donated it to the city. The architectural firm of Heins and LaFarge, whose other credits included the original stations of the IRT subway, the Bronx Zoo and the Cathedral of St. John the Divine, designed a modest Renaissance Revival structure. Situated on a central green, the handsome Poppenhusen Branch was built at a total cost of $30,114.30, by far the lowest cost of all the Carnegies—indeed, of all libraries in the borough. Later that year the Carnegie library in Astoria opened, an unusual brick and terra-cotta edifice praised for its spacious children's room, toilets, steam heat and perfect ventilation.

Unlike the generous citizens of College Point, the Man family, developers of Richmond Hill and Kew Gardens, sold their site at the intersection of Hillside Avenue and Lefferts Boulevard to the city for $12,000. The Jamaica firm of Tuthill & Higgins designed both the Astoria and Richmond Hill branches. The most contentious process occurred in Elmhurst. The site selection committee, which included Borough President Joseph Cassidy and Charles V. Fornes, President of the Board of Aldermen, rejected four free sites in the emerging neighborhood, including one offered by Cord Meyer, primary developer of Elmhurst and the man responsible for changing the name from Newtown; they elected instead to pay a political crony $10,000 for the current site on Broadway.

While the Carnegies received much-deserved attention, the system was slow to add branches in other neighborhoods since that depended upon municipal funding. Only the Bayside Branch on Bell Boulevard and the Broadway Branch in Astoria opened by 1906. In retrospect it is surprising that Jamaica did not receive a Carnegie, for it was not only one of the oldest villages in Queens, but also the emerging center of transportation and commerce.

In November 1906, the Jamaica Branch opened in an antebellum school house, and in 1911 it moved to Colonial Hall, an 1843 academy on Jamaica Avenue.

The Queens Borough Public Library was incorporated in May 1907, changing its name from the Queens Borough Library and permitting "libraries in the Borough of Queens of the City of New York, to convey their property thereto." On October 18, the City of New York transferred control of the Queens libraries to a new, independent board of trustees, while maintaining responsibility for the system's financial support.

Colonial Hall, 1911. This 1843 academy on Jamaica Avenue was the home of the Jamaica Branch and the Library's administrative offices from 1911 to 1923.

Through the first decade of the 20th Century, the city's largest borough developed at a measured pace, as did the Library. In the following decades, however, changes came in rapid succession, and the Queens Borough Public Library would be hard pressed to serve a population increasing at a phenomenal rate.

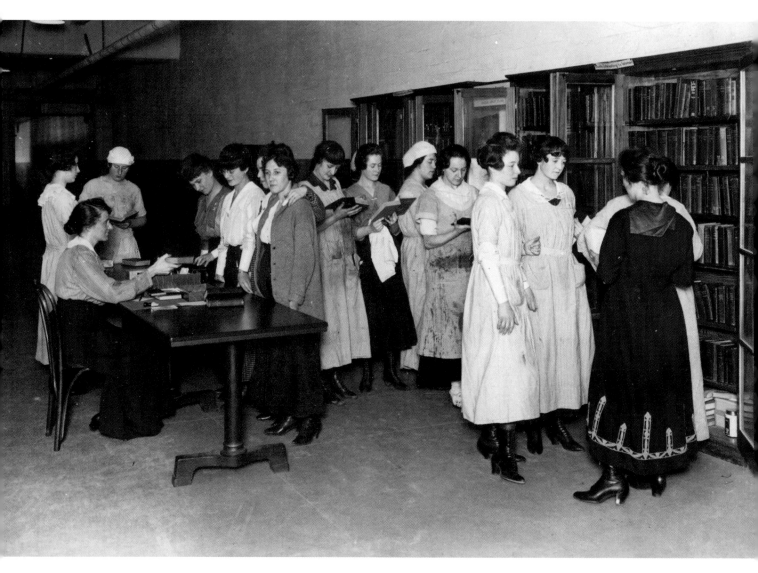

In 1916, a traveling station with over 700 volumes was established at the Loose Wiles Biscuit factory in Long Island City. A librarian charged out books each day during lunch hour.

To Serve the Booming Borough

The completion of new transportation links with Manhattan had an immediate impact on the pace of development. In 1909, the Queensboro Bridge opened, and the magnificent new Penn Station was completed the next year, bringing the newly electrified Long Island Rail Road directly into Manhattan. By 1917, elevated transit lines stretched to Jamaica, Corona, Ridgewood and Astoria, quickening construction along those routes. During the Roaring Twenties, Queens was arguably the fastest growing county in the nation, with an international reputation for model housing and planned communities, including Forest Hills Gardens, Jackson Heights, Sunnyside Gardens, the Mathews Model Flats and the Metropolitan Life Houses. Everywhere truck gardens yielded to housing.

In 1911, Queens Library relocated its administrative offices from Hunters Point to Colonial Hall in Jamaica. Commuter traffic through Hunters Point had declined precipitously since 1909, while Jamaica was rising in importance because of the Long Island Rail Road and the streetcar network which extended into Brooklyn and Nassau. Stylish shops, office buildings and movie palaces lined Jamaica Avenue, which assumed greater importance in the life of the borough.

To stretch limited resources in the face of mounting demands for services, the Library embraced imaginative and innovative methods. Deposit collections were placed in the care of community groups, fire companies and the like; traveling libraries were set up in factories, cigar stores, schools and real estate offices, where a librarian arrived weekly to charge out books and to bring a fresh selection. No place was too humble, and no segment of the population was considered unworthy of the institution's attention. Many traveling stations became permanent branches in rented storefronts. By 1915, there were 20 branches and 18 traveling stations, including collections in the men's and women's jails. The annual city appropriation was $155,000; the system held 214,000 volumes and circulation topped 1.5 million.

Story hour at the Seaside Branch, 1910.

Early on, children received special attention. The Library's Department of Children's Work was started in early 1908 under Harriot Hassler, who visited each of the branches to bring seasonal poems and pictures and to observe the young women on staff. In 1911, story hours became a regularly scheduled activity in each branch, and over the decades this remained the Library's most consistently popular activity. In 1912, the department reported that children used the library in summer when it was too hot to play outside, "and nearly all Branches have had very full reading rooms on bitter cold days when the Library is one of the few comfortable places accessible." It noted especially the use of the branches by 12- to 14-year olds "because they've no place else that is equally wholesome to go," adding that it would be a real loss to the community if the library were closed in the evenings.

To increase circulation and invite a wider circle of residents into its branches, the Library initiated a series of clever outreach measures: distributing Italian-language circulars in Italian neighborhoods; sending lists of books appropriate for each grade to public and parochial schools; listing books suggested by the plant superintendent of a College Point business on pay envelopes; posting a list of books "For Mothers" at the City Milk Station in Astoria; printing lists of "Books for Business Men" on postcards sold at the East River ferry terminals; and sending slides depicting the local branch and children's story hour to movie houses. Typical slides read, "There are Polish books at the Public Library. Free to All" and "The Public Library is the working man's college. Use it."

Throughout its early years, the Library addressed the needs of immigrants and their children. When the First World War began in 1914, the great flood of immigration slowed to barely a trickle. Nor did it resume after the Armistice in November 1918, for Congress closed the "Golden Door," restricting immigration for the first time in the nation's history (with the notable exception of the 1882 Chinese Exclusion Act).

Children in the Ridgewood Station, 1910. It was designated a branch on March 17, 1911.

The United States entered the war in April 1917, and the libraries were soon hit by staff shortages as many employees took other positions paying higher wages. The Library contributed to the war effort by providing space for the Red Cross, hosting Liberty Loan drives and organizing book drives for servicemen. The war caused hardships on the home front, of course. Because of the coal shortage, branches closed for "heatless Mondays" in early 1918, with some shuttered for weeks at a time.

The patriotic hysteria of the day resulted in the only overt act of censorship in the Library's history. All German-language books were withdrawn from circulation, and all foreign-language volumes were temporarily transferred to the Central Reserve Collection in Jamaica. After the war the fervor for censorship quickly ebbed. In 1919, for example, a Queens newspaper reported a controversy regarding reproductions of Renaissance paintings hung in the public library: "Despite the protests of the W.C.T.U. [Women's Christian Temperance Union] and the Purity league, the nude pictures in the public library at Elmhurst will remain there. The director of the library guaranteed that they are all examples of acknowledged art and that until the library trustees order their removal, they will stay where they are."

During the 1920s, the population of Queens soared from 469,042 to 1,079,129. Serving the booming borough strained the Library's limited resources. The city, which supplied almost all of the institution's funding, was reluctant to increase its budget. Still, stations were established in new neighborhoods, though at times residents had to take matters into their own hands. The Library set up a traveling station in St. Albans in 1920, and the next year the community's Mothers' Club purchased an old lunch wagon parked in a vacant lot for use as a branch. Five years later the community rented a storefront, and residents even donated dozens of books.

The Library established its own library school in 1927. Four classes graduated by 1931, when the school was closed.

Another problem was the retention of talented personnel, particularly as higher-paying office work beckoned elsewhere in the city. A 1922 editorial in the *Long Island City Daily Star* supported the demand of the Queens librarians for higher salaries, pointing out that they received hundreds of dollars less than their counterparts in Manhattan and Brooklyn: "The work of a librarian requires intelligence, wide knowledge and special training. And it is work in which a fine type of young womanhood is engaged. In the last few years many employes [*sic*] in the library service of Queens have resigned their positions to enter more lucrative lines of endeavor, and each year it is becoming increasingly difficult to get the right kind of young women to undertake examinations to fill vacancies." To remedy the situation, the Library established its own library school in 1927, graduating four classes by 1931. It was closed that year because the American Library Association refused to accredit any program not affiliated with a degree-granting institution.

In March 1926, the Board of Estimate rejected the Library's request for $610,000 in construction funds, even rescinding a $345,000 appropriation for construction of the Central Library in Jamaica. In response, the Library implemented austerity measures, reducing hours from 72 to 48 hours a week for large branches and from 48 to 40 hours a week in smaller branches, accepting no new registrations and limiting borrowing privileges to "bona fide residents of Queens Borough." An increase for 1927 fund-

The Central
Library under
construction,
1928.

ed 37 new positions and restoration of full service, but this was not the last time city officials would see a tempting target in the library budget.

The Queens Library dedicated its limited resources toward making the greatest number of books available to the greatest number of residents, rather than constructing handsome branch buildings, which would have directly benefitted only a small portion of the borough. During this decade of phenomenal urbanization, Queens Library erected only three buildings. The Woodhaven Branch opened in January 1924, using the last of the Carnegie money. There were 1,271 volumes when it opened and 1,000 more were soon added, but within a month librarians reported there were only 11 children's books left on the shelves. In 1929, the Ridgewood Branch opened, the first built entirely with city funds.

The grandest architectural achievement of the decade was the erection of the four-story Renaissance Revival Central Library on Parsons Boulevard. The cornerstone-laying ceremony took place on October 23, 1928, in a misty rain before a crowd of about 500, most of them school children who had marched there. Neither Borough President Bernard M. Patten nor Mayor James J. Walker managed to attend. The mayor did find his way to Queens for the dedication a year later, though. One observer described a "vivid picture of happy, intelligent men and women anxious to see a truly modern democratic institution." Above the children's entrance were carved the words "What greater gift or better can we offer to the state than if we teach and train up youth." Above the main entrance was a phrase by William Wordsworth: "These hoards of wealth you can unlock at will." In 1966, the Library moved into a new home, and the Parsons Boulevard building became the Family Court. Sadly, those inspiring words were chiseled off.

A NEW BUILDING FOR THE
GLENDALE BRANCH
OF
THE QUEENS BOROUGH
PUBLIC LIBRARY
WILL BE ERECTED ON THIS SITE BY
UNITED STATES
WORKS PROGRESS
ADMINISTRATION
Project Nº 65-97-97

Depression and War

In late October 1929, the Wall Street bubble burst. The stock market crash brought an immediate end to the decade of prosperity, the "financial drunk" as humorist Will Rogers put it, and ushered in the nation's worst economic crisis. The Great Depression brought unprecedented levels of unemployment and the nearly total collapse of the private sector. The jobless soon overwhelmed all sources of private charity. Families faced bitter choices among food, shelter and other necessities. Evictions and foreclosures, often enforced by city marshals, became tragically common. The diary of one Queens man speaks with poignant eloquence of his own plight in September 1933: "We are flat cold stony broke and no place in the world to get any money. Have been living mainly on boxes of food from the Red Cross and received the last one yesterday as they have stopped giving them out. We owe 6 months Rent. Resources all drained. I wonder what will happen now? God help us." What happened is explained in an entry from December 1935: "Two years on the WPA [Works Progress Administration] job. Grateful for it but hope to get on my own soon." What happened to him was the New Deal.

Franklin Delano Roosevelt won a landslide victory over incumbent President Herbert Hoover in November 1932, promising a "New Deal" for the American people. His administration represented a powerful break with the past. For the first time the federal government would fund local projects in cities and states. In Queens alone between 1933 and 1940, federal dollars built the Triborough and Whitestone Bridges; the Queens-Midtown Tunnel; the Cross Island, Interboro and Grand Central Parkways; Queens Borough Hall and Court House; the Queensbridge

The Glendale Branch under construction, 1935. This was one of many public works projects completed in Queens during the New Deal.

and South Jamaica housing projects; schools and post offices; and sewage treatment plants. The New Deal also financed construction of La Guardia Airport, Astoria Park and Pool, Juniper Valley Park, the Rockaway Beach boardwalk, Riis Park and the Marine Parkway Bridge and, finally, the 1939 World's Fair, the "World of Tomorrow." Only the massive infusion of federal funds kept men and women on the job, while providing a major customer for the construction industry and its suppliers.

Before FDR's New Deal began writing checks, however, the Queens Borough Public Library confronted the crisis on its own. In 1930, Mayor Walker christened the first book bus, *Pioneer*. The daughter of municipal budget director Charles L. Kohler had the honor of breaking the bottle containing water from Jamaica, Flushing and Little Neck Bays, the East River and the Atlantic Ocean (it was during Prohibition, after all!) on the bumper. In October, the *Pioneer* traveled to Albany for the New York Library Association conference and called on then-Governor Franklin Delano Roosevelt, who inspected the vehicle and received a library card.

The first book bus at a stop in Laurelton, 1930.

The *Pioneer* carried 2,000 volumes to the borough's outlying neighborhoods and was equipped with a radio to broadcast the children's stories read over municipal radio station WNYC. Covering 150 miles each week, the *Pioneer* made stops at 12 public and parochial schools, seven street intersections and two transit terminals. In April 1934, 450 books were loaned in an hour and a half at the Baisley Park stop. Such enthusiasm convinced the Library to open a branch there the next year. The *Pioneer* was retired in February 1938 due to its "dilapidated condition," replaced a year later by *Progress*, so-christened by Mayor Fiorello La Guardia, who used the occasion to obtain a library card, listing his occupation as "civic worker."

Despite the hardships of the time, the Library celebrated the opening of its Long Island Collection in January 1932. The division's origins go back to December 1911, when the trustees voted $500 "to build up a special collection of books, maps, documents, etc. relating to Long Island." The 1873 Beers *Atlas of Long Island*, a nearly complete run of the *Long Island Democrat* from 1845 forward, Onderdonk's *Queens County in Olden Times*, and Prince's *Short Treatise on Horticulture* were among the first materials acquired. In 1916, Chief Librarian Jessie Hume appealed to Queens residents for donations of historical documents. "The public library is the place for such a collection," she said, "and with the co-operation of the old families of the borough, a collection could be made which would surpass those of the New York Historical Society and the Long Island Historical Society." In 1939, through the generosity of Jamaica merchant Henry Gertz, the Library acquired a great prize: the original 1686 Dongan Patent for the Town of Jamaica.

The worsening depression forced drastic reductions in municipal spending, but the cuts came at a time when many New Yorkers depended on their local libraries more than ever. In January 1933, the *New York Times* reported a change in reading tastes among Queens Library users, noting renewed interest in many old-fashioned arts which had fallen into disuse during the period of prosperity. One librarian observed, "Readers evidently are in pursuit of methods for making useful and artistic objects for home decoration. Within the last few years a keen appreciation of hand-made articles has been awakened. Handicraft books, giving practical instructions for making these articles, have been in great demand. Books containing suggestions for amusement for a family group at home also have been found useful by persons affected by the depression." For some, the free public library was undoubtedly the sum total of their entertainment budget, and surely many people took advantage of the warmth of the library buildings in winter because they had no money to heat their own homes.

Bookbinders employed by the Library through the Civil Works Administration, 1934.

The New Deal enabled the institution to keep librarians on the payroll and maintain generous hours, and made possible the hiring of dozens of clerks and bookbinders. The Library's report on the occasion of its 40th anniversary in 1936 noted: "If it had not been for the assistance of the WPA clerks and librarians assigned to the Library, many of its services would necessarily have been cut short. With their help all essential activities have been maintained, and through the securing of many workers trained in special fields much additional work has been accomplished which would not otherwise have been possible."

Federal dollars paid for the expansion of the Central Library and the Richmond Hill, Astoria, Far Rockaway and Ridgewood branches, but surprisingly the WPA erected only one branch in Queens during the New Deal, a handsome Renaissance revival structure in Glendale dedicated in January 1937. The neighborhood's first traveling station had been set up in a shoe store in 1911 and moved into a rented storefront in 1915. Residents had petitioned the Library for a full-service branch for more than 15 years, but only the unique circumstances of the Great Depression made it a reality.

Interior, Woodside Branch, 1937.

When the Woodside Branch finally opened in 1937, four years after the building was completed, the public could admire Buk Ulrich's murals in the children's room illustrating the history of writing, and "The Acquisition of Long Island" by James D. Brooks in the main reading room. Other WPA murals were created in Astoria, Flushing and Richmond Hill. Unfortunately, the Flushing murals were destroyed when the 1906 Carnegie library was torn down in the early '50s, and the Woodside murals were lost during renovations in the '60s. Sadly, Max Spivak's circus murals in the children's room in Astoria have been badly damaged. "The Story of Richmond Hill," contrasting an ideal, wholesome suburb with an unhealthy and dreary urban neighborhood, happily is still intact in the Richmond Hill Branch.

The Second World War began in September 1939, and the federal government immediately shifted its priorities from domestic employment to defense. Responding to the global crisis and the likelihood of America's involvement, the Library put together a special collection called "The America You Defend." Librarian Francis D. Stark commented, "How many people really know and appreciate the country they are now working to defend? If we are called upon to fight for our country, what will we be fighting for? Democracy can best be preserved by educating the people to their country's greatness." A list of books on safeguarding democracy was sent to all high school teachers and college professors in the borough.

When America entered the war in December 1941, Queens Library Director Louis Bailey stated, "Books, the inheritance and the heritage, carry onward the messages of liberty, democratic freedom and the eternal hope of a higher and better way of life. To defend that spirit, the personnel of the Queens Public Library is ready for every duty and will meet any emergency to the limit of its resources."

"The Story of Writing," WPA murals installed in the children's room of the Woodside Branch, 1937.

Library Director Louis Bailey and a patriotic exhibit in the Central Library, 1942.

Director Bailey was named national chairman of the Library Bond campaign, coordinating bond drives in libraries across the country. The staff responded to the challenge much as it had when America entered the First World War in 1917, hosting bond drives and raising money for the Red Cross. During the tumultuous war years, there were relatively few changes in library services. After 1945, however, Queens experienced another growth spurt, and an unprecedented construction campaign brought new library buildings to neighborhoods across the borough.

Story hour in the children's room of the Central Library, 1940.

New Branches,
New Neighborhoods

The Library's 50th anniversary in 1946 occasioned a gala dinner at the Hotel Commodore drawing 500 guests (at $5 a person). Author Christopher Morley presented a collection of 15 letters by William Cullen Bryant to the Library, and the proceedings were broadcast live over the municipal radio station WNYC. During that anniversary year, of course, each branch across the borough hosted its own celebrations, often involving children from all the public and parochial schools in the neighborhood.

Over its first half century, Queens Library had grown to 44 branches, in addition to the grand Central Library in Jamaica and the ever-dependable bookmobile. There were over 800,000 items in the collection, and circulation topped 2.7 million. From 1940 to 1960 the borough's population rose by 500,000 to 1.8 million. During that time large-scale public housing projects rose in Long Island City and the Rockaways: Queensbridge (1940), South Jamaica (1940), Woodside (1949), Astoria (1951), Ravenswood (1951), Arverne (1951), Redfern (1953) and Hammel (1955). Vast stretches of eastern Queens had resisted subdivision until the post-war decades, but single-family detached houses and garden apartments soon dotted the landscape. In the 1950s, Jamaica Avenue remained the primary shopping area, attracting consumers from Brooklyn and Nassau who annually pumped many millions of dollars into retail shops. Gradually, though, more and more shoppers shifted to new suburban malls.

The model community of Glen Oaks Village was a garden apartment complex of 2,864 units near the Nassau

The Library opened a branch in the Arverne Houses, a public housing project, in 1951.

border. Construction of the two-story brick buildings began in 1945, and the first residents, many of them veterans, arrived in October 1947. The Library's bookmobile began regular stops at the new neighborhood at the same time; in February 1950 a branch opened on Union Turnpike. The Library also rushed to bring service to Fresh Meadows, the New York Life Insurance Company's 166-acre mixed housing development. A branch opened there in November 1949, just months after the first residents moved in. The new neighborhoods quickly gained library services, of course, but so did the housing projects. A branch opened in the Queensbridge Houses in 1949, and within two years the Ravenswood, Arverne, Woodside and Pomonok projects also boasted their own. The community around the South Jamaica Houses, originally an integrated project completed in 1940, had first requested a facility in 1947; the South Jamaica Branch opened in its own building in October 1961.

Unlike the 1920s, when the Library barely kept up with demand by renting storefronts and, finally, running the book bus, the post-war years brought the first large-scale construction program in the institution's history. Much of the construction took place after Harold Tucker became director in 1954. Until his death in 1973, Tucker

ON THIS SITE
WILL BE ERECTED THE NE
SOUTH JAMAICA BRAN
OF THE
QUEENS BOROUGH PUBLIC LIBI

Ground-breaking for the South Jamaica Branch, 1961.

was the driving force behind the modernization or replacement of storefront facilities.

As 1964 came to a close, the system consisted of 53 branches and three bookmobiles, in addition to the Central Library, with holdings of 1,985,019 volumes and 18,317 recordings. The Queens Borough Public Library could look to the future with confidence. Several new branches were going up and others were on the drafting table. And construction of the long-awaited new Central Library on Merrick Boulevard was right on schedule.

During the fiscal crisis in the 1970s, the Library endured a series of
drastic budget cuts. Most branches were open only three days a week.
Here children protest in front of the Arverne Branch, 1975.

Changes and
Challenges

Two crucial events in the history of the Queens Library took place in Washington, D.C. in 1965. As part of President Lyndon Johnson's "Great Society," Congress passed the Library Services and Construction Act (LSCA), which funded the expansion of library service across the country, and the Immigration Reform Act, which abolished national quotas and reopened the "Golden Door." The effect on Queens was as unexpected as it was dynamic. The borough became the most culturally, racially, linguistically and religiously diverse place in the nation—and probably the world.

Demographic changes in the post-war decades presented the system with additional challenges, as many black families moved from the older neighborhoods of Manhattan and Brooklyn to better quality housing in Queens. In the wake of the "great migration," it was clear that urban libraries needed federal assistance. The LSCA specifically addressed that issue, even as the urban crisis appeared on the horizon. Director Harold Tucker was well aware of these issues. In 1963, he chaired the American Library Association's "Access to Libraries" committee, studying library facilities in the segregated South. He astutely used that experience to advocate the construction of new branches in underserved or impoverished Queens neighborhoods.

The civil rights movement compelled all Americans to face what Swedish sociologist Gunnar Myrdal called "the American Dilemma." Attention to the needs of the borough's underserved neighborhoods was certainly an important dimension of the Library's strategy in the '60s and '70s. Adhering to its tradition of innovation and inclusion, the Library established "Operation Headstart" in March 1965, six months before inception of the federal Head Start program. The Library's program addressed the needs of pre-schoolers by bringing books to bookless homes, while also training parents to help their children read. College students working as library aides canvassed the South Jamaica Houses and nearby blocks, bringing 300 children into the program in the small South Jamaica Branch. Predictably, circulation increased rapidly. In 1967, the library created the "Library-Go-Round," a book bus designed for small children, later adding the "Tell-a-Tale Trailer" for older children and the "Library in Action Teenmobile."

Above and right: With initial funding of $134,568, "Operation Headstart" began on March 3, 1965. The program introduced pre-schoolers to books, and included special training for parents and programs for teens. Here mothers and children take part in the program at the Rockaway Beach Branch.

Another remarkable achievement was the Langston Hughes Community Library and Cultural Center in Corona, which opened on April 7, 1969, largely funded through an LSCA grant. Local activists encouraged the Library to acquire a boarded-up storefront—originally a Woolworth's, then a toy warehouse—and the project finally went forward. The Center proved an oasis indeed. Although a professional librarian was assigned to the new facility, the rest of the staff came from the immediate neighborhood. According to an early

brochure, materials included books, periodicals and records aimed at improving the "self-image" of the community, "a basic African and Black history collection," and various works "for self-improvement and home study." There was no card catalogue, and no fines were imposed. According to 27-year old Tyrone Bryant, elected by the community to supervise the facility, "The library is supposed to be free. You can trust people who built a library to bring back the books."

The Great Society also funded an unprecedented building spree, contributing toward the construction of modern buildings from one end of Queens to the other.

The record collection in the Langston Hughes Community Library, 1970.

The centerpiece, of course, was the new Central Library on Merrick Boulevard, which replaced the elegant but cramped home on Parsons Boulevard. Built at a total cost of $5.7 million, it was dedicated on April 11, 1966, the first major urban library in the nation with all public services on one floor. A visit to the new facility was one of the highlights of that year's American Library Association Convention in Manhattan.

But the first hints of the looming fiscal crisis tempered the optimism evident in the celebrations. In March 1969, New York City's budget director requested that the Queens Library submit a plan to implement a cut of more than 20%. Queens Library users generated thousands of letters in protest, and demonstrations were staged outside several neighborhood branches. At the North Hills Branch, which had opened in 1964, children carried signs proclaiming, "We got a snow job in February, Don't Book us now" and "Last on the list for snow removal … First on the list for library removal." One even quoted Benjamin Franklin: "An Investment in knowledge pays the best dividend." The mention of snow on the placards referred to

the blizzard earlier that year, when many Queens streets remained unplowed while Manhattan thoroughfares were cleared repeatedly. Known derisively as the "Lindsay snowstorm" (after the incumbent mayor), it seemed to represent all the differences between the swinging city and family-centered Queens. The loud public outcry helped reduce the cuts from the originally proposed $1.7 million to "only" $300,000, but this brief episode foreshadowed the city's worsening financial state. As long as new facilities opened, however, the future seemed solid.

In the 1970s, branches long planned and under construction were ultimately completed, often after years of delays, but system-wide maintenance suffered. By 1975, the fiscal crisis forced unfortunate choices on the city; service cutbacks and deferred maintenance characterized all aspects of municipal government. During the Great Depression, FDR's New Deal had prevented devastating

Architect's rendering of the new Central Library, 1966.

42

layoffs and branches had remained open six days a week. During the fiscal crisis of the mid-1970s, however, the federal government did not step in, a decision summarized in the famous *Daily News* headline, "Ford to City: Drop Dead." Library service citywide was brutally curtailed, with branches open only three days a week.

In 1975, Library Director Milton Byam announced that the Glendale Branch, then undergoing renovation, and 10 others were slated for permanent closing as the "least used" in the system. Brenda Thomas, a fifth-grader in South Ozone Park, wrote in protest: "Every Saturday I go to the library and read and read. I really go there to get away from the house but I really like to read. But if you don't open the libraries I'll be so hurt inside and very sad." Another schoolgirl complained: "Now, when you were younger, did they close the libraries? Did they have school strikes? Well, that's what they're doing to us youngsters." Public outcry and a federal lawsuit by the National Association for the Advancement of Colored People (NAACP) blocked the plan. NAACP attorney James I. Meyerson contended the action would violate the rights of minorities because eight of the 11 branches were in black neighborhoods.

There were protests from Ravenswood to Arverne. While no branches were shuttered for good, hours were sharply cut. For instance, the Glendale Branch reopened in August 1976 after a three-year renovation, with a new roof, windows, heating system and air conditioning, but was only open a total of 22 hours a week. Some branches were paired with others, and their staffs merged; Steinway and Sunnyside, for example, were open on alternate days, served by the same librarians. Some frustrated citizens took matters into their own hands, staging demonstrations and in a few cases, even temporarily occupying branch buildings.

In a letter to the *Long Island Press* in early 1977 about cuts to the library, Rachel Sapienza of Astoria wrote: "I am 13 years old and never realized how useful the libraries really are until the hours were cut. My neighborhood's library is only open three days a week. I understand that in these times there is very little money, but I think it is a

crime for us kids to be denied a form of education. We must remember that the future lies in our hands and the library is the best place for us to learn about many areas."

The opening of the South Hollis Branch, 1974.

New branches opened, but each completed project seemed a bit closer to the end of an era than the fulfillment of optimistic expectations. The East Flushing Branch opened in September 1977, delayed almost two years because of staff cuts and reduced operating expenses; Bellerose opened in February 1978, almost a year after the building was completed; and Hillcrest finally opened in April 1980, six years after work was finished. There were horrible construction delays, with work suspended for years at a time. The bad news just continued. In 1978, the Woodhaven Branch was severely damaged by a fire set by two teenage vandals. It reopened two years later.

Libraries had seemed a soft target during the fiscal crisis, but the political fallout was severe. With a semblance

POPULATION, BRANCHES AND CIRCULATION

1900-1990

Year	New York City	Queens	QBPL Branches*	Circulation
1900	3,347,202	152,999	3	68,339
1910	4,766,883	284,041	17	749,064
1920	5,620,048	469,042	21	1,826,768
1930	6,930,446	1,079,129	41	2,617,939
1940	7,454,995	1,297,634	47	4,356,968
1950	7,891,957	1,550,849	49	3,479,226
1960	7,781,984	1,809,578	51	6,966,139
1970	7,894,862	1,986,473	56	7,592,572
1980	7,071,639	1,891,325	56	5,852,476
1990	7,332,564	1,951,598	63	13,202,363

*including the Central Library, sub-branches and community stations, but not traveling stations, school stations, hospital service or book bus stops.

of budgetary health re-established in the 1980s, the construction and maintenance problems of the previous decade began to recede, albeit slowly. Five years of severe budget cuts could hardly be redressed overnight. Political pressures also eased, but the 1983 proposed city budget called for cuts of $5.6 million for libraries, out of a total budget of $16.7 billion. City Council member Edward Sadowsky, chair of the Finance Committee, complained, "I think it is wrong, and it ought to stop. It's been a cynical game played by OMB [Office of Management and Budget] ...they know what kind of uproar will ensue." He pointed out that during each of the last three budget cycles the Council and the Board of Estimate restored the cuts. "Everybody will be able to pat each other on the back and say what a wonderful job we have done."

Queens Library

Queens Borough Public Library

LIGHTING THE WAY
1896 • 1996

About the Library:	Information Resources:
What's happening at Queens Library?	*InfoLinQ*: Search the Library's Catalog
What's special about Queens Library?	Community Services Database
The branch libraries	Periodical and Reference Databases
The Central Library	Government Information Resources
Library programs & services	Subject guides to Library materials
Facts about the Queens Library	Discover Queens, New York
In the Queens Library Gallery...	Explore the Internet

Please read about the Queens Library Foundation's *Future's Fund*

? Home Look it up! Events Branches Central Internet Programs Special Queens Home

Visitors are obliged to familiarize themselves with the Library Internet Policy for Public Use and Guidelines for Public Use of the Queens Library InfoLinQ before they proceed.

The Library
of the Future

The Library emerged like a phoenix from the fiscal crisis. Appointed in August 1979, Director Constance B. Cooke took steps which re-established the institution's central role in urban life. By 1983, Queens had the third-highest circulation in the nation, surpassing the Brooklyn and Chicago systems; the next year it topped the New York Public Library to rank second behind Los Angeles. The Queens Borough Public Library celebrated its 90th anniversary in 1986 as the most heavily used system in the nation, with total circulation of 10,519,034. By 1996, its Centennial year, circulation topped 15 million items, as more than eight million people came through its doors.

The dynamic spirit which had characterized Queens Library for its entire history was once more in evidence after the terrible years of the late 1970s. In 1981, branches with the lowest circulation received additional funding to purchase paperbacks which reflected the reading tastes of the neighborhood; in Corona, borrowing increased 83% within a year. The Library also inaugurated the "bookstore look." Sadly, in 1982 the Library installed anti-theft devices in all branches, surely an admission that societal norms had declined; the loss of books was immediately reduced, freeing up scarce funds for additional staff and materials. But perhaps times had not changed so much after all. In 1911, 544 books were stolen, but after one culprit was convicted of stealing a library book, others voluntarily returned their outstanding books; some anonymously left volumes on the steps.

The Queens Library's home page on the World Wide Web, 1996.

In the '80s the Library loaned recordings and videos in ever-increasing numbers. The Art and Music Department had begun to circulate records in 1947, but figures skyrocketed with the introduction of cassettes and compact discs.

The library had begun a film collection in 1954, offering educational and government films to community groups, but no one then anticipated the advent of videos, bringing classic films (and some not-so-classic films) into the home. Videos were first available in a few branches in 1984, and within only three years circulation reached 422,000.

It is unlikely that the construction binge of the 1960s and 1970s will ever be repeated, for there were now libraries everywhere. With the exception of residents of Breezy Point at the tip of the Rockaway peninsula, no one in Queens lived more than a mile from a branch.

The first great event in the institution's second century will be the opening of the new Flushing Regional Branch, the fourth library on the site since 1891. Designed by Polshek and Partners, this innovative structure will house the technology essential for the library of the future. The need was acute, for since 1986 Flushing had been the system's most heavily used branch. A librarian once reported: "The tables in the reference room and lending room are

Architect's rendering of the new Flushing Branch, scheduled for completion in 1998. This is the fourth library building on the site.

utilized from the moment the doors open to the dimming of the lights, to signify closing time. The ultimate in reader frustration was witnessed when a patron was discovered studying while sitting on the staircase leading to the auditorium. We have wall-to-wall children..."

The InfoLinQ station in the Central Library, 1995.

Another new development was the technological revolution. Where once there was an imposing card catalogue listing every volume in neatly alphabetized drawers, now there were computer terminals. InfoLinQ (Information On-Line at Queens Library) was dedicated at the Central Library in October 1993. For the first time, readers were instantly able to learn the location and availability of materials in the collection. On March 19, 1996, its 100th anniversary to the day, the Library entered cyberspace, unveiling its own home page on the World Wide Web (http://www.queens.lib.ny.us) and offering free public access to the Internet. Using a computer anywhere in the world, users could access the Library's own database around the clock. In its early decades, the Library democratized the printed word; it has since widened access to the wealth of information available electronically.

This commitment had a price tag, however, and came at a time when support from all levels of government was being reduced. To bridge this gap, the Queens Library Foundation was established by the Library's Board of Trustees in 1988 to raise the institution's profile with, and create financial support from, corporations, foundations and private citizens. Its first grant was from the J. M. Kaplan Fund to open the Flushing Branch on Sundays. A grant from the National Endowment for the Humanities in 1995 funded an exhibit about the life and work of black inventor Lewis Latimer—Civil War veteran, Flushing resident and colleague of Thomas Edison. That was the first exhibit in the Central Library's new Gallery, created to house cultural and historical exhibits. Within its first four years, the Foundation had secured more than 11,000 financial donations.

At its heart, however, the mission of the Queens Library will remain the same well into the 21st Century; that is, providing reading materials and information for the borough's increasingly diverse population. Books, music, and videos were available in more than 40 languages, assuring that newcomers could embrace the Library as their own. But while children eagerly ex-

The line to register for free ESL classes in the Jackson Heights Branch, 1982.

plored their local branches, adults who do not understand English had to be encouraged. Once brought into the library, though, they discovered free English-as-a-Second-Language (ESL) classes. Under the auspices of the New Americans Program, these classes and other cultural programs eased adjustment to life in the United States. In 1993, more than 3,000 adults were registered for classes, representing 82 countries and speaking 51 languages.

This outstanding effort, however, did not address one of the country's most pressing, persistent and intractable problems: adult illiteracy, called the "silent scandal" by historian Richard C. Wade. One out of five adults in the United States, the overwhelming majority of them native-born Americans, was functionally illiterate. This situation had dire consequences for employment, welfare and even the soul of our democracy. Since 1977, the Library had offered one-to-one tutoring for illiterate adults and, even before then, parents were brought in through Head Start programs for pre-schoolers. Parents were thus learning alongside their children. Classes for new readers will undoubtedly remain an important part of the Library's mission as it enters its second century.

As ever, it is the discovery of the public library by children that continually energizes the staff and keeps the institution vibrant. On June 15, 1994, the St. Albans Chapter of the Friends of the Library honored winners of their "Dear Library" essay contest at PS 36. In his winning essay, third-grader Jason Johnson wrote: "This year I got so bored. So I went to the library. The library really changed my life. This year I read 32 books from the library. Reading is good for you. In fact, today I'm going to the library to get five books."

Queens Library...

...has the highest circulation in the nation

...serves nearly two million people

...offers more than 16,000 free programs each year

...is your community information and cultural center

THE QUEENS BOROUGH PUBLIC LIBRARY SYSTEM

A branch directory featured this system map showing Queens Library locations throughout the borough in 1996.

CHIEF LIBRARIANS/DIRECTORS OF THE QUEENS BOROUGH PUBLIC LIBRARY

Jessie Hume	December 13, 1907 – March 24, 1919
John C. Atwater	February 1, 1920 – January 31, 1925
Owen J. Dever	April 1, 1925 – May 31, 1935
Louis J. Bailey	January 2, 1936 – January 1, 1954
Harold W. Tucker	August 1, 1954 – April 4, 1973
Milton S. Byam	June 1, 1974 – June 30, 1979
Constance B. Cooke	August 1, 1979 – July 31, 1994
Gary E. Strong	September 6, 1994 –Present

Children in the Ozone Park Branch, ca. 1910. Sponsored by Brooklyn Union.

An Illustrated Chronology of the Queens Borough Public Library

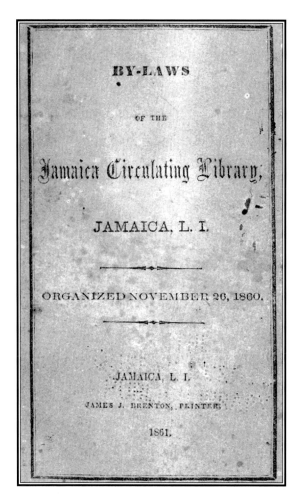

The Jamaica Circulating Library was established on November 26, 1860, two years after the founding of the Flushing Library Association. Shares of stock were $5, with an annual assessment of 50¢ per share. According to the by-laws, "Any person may become a subscriber to the Association by paying one Dollar for which he shall be entitled to the use of the Library and Reading Rooms for one year." A lifetime membership was $20.

Left: In 1880, wealthy Manhattanites founded the New York Free Circulating Library. They viewed the library as "one of the most progressive means toward the moral and intellectual elevation of the masses." Andrew Carnegie became one of the trustees in 1893. Shown here is the Lord & Taylor department store at Broadway and 20th Street in 1872. Founded in 1826, the city's oldest specialty store was one of the fashionable shops along Manhattan's Ladies Mile, which stretched from 14th to 23rd Streets. For many years, co-founder Samuel Lord lived in Newtown, Queens. Sponsored by Lord & Taylor.

Left: The Queens County Savings Bank was founded in 1873 in Flushing and occupied this building on Northern Boulevard until 1911. Sponsored by Queens County Savings Bank.

Facing page: The Flushing Library moved into a small Baptist Church at Main Street and Kissena Boulevard (originally Jaggar and Jamaica) in 1891. This was the first of four library buildings on the site. This view dates from about 1903. Sponsored by Flushing Savings Bank.

Above: The Flushing Library was opened to the public as a free circulating library in 1884, though it remained a private institution. Pictured here is Main Street looking toward Northern Boulevard, ca. 1880. Sponsored by Queens County Savings Bank.

The Shakespeare Club of Queens [Village] organized a public library in 1896. It merged with the Queens Borough Library in January 1901. This view of the Queens Branch on Railroad Avenue dates from 1910. Sponsored by Antun's Caterers of Queens Village.

In May 1901, the Nelson Branch moved from its first home at 26 Jackson Avenue to 101 East Avenue in Hunters Point where it remained until 1912. In this classic progressive era photograph, the barefoot boy on the sidewalk is "rushing the growler," fetching a bucket of beer from a local saloon for nearby workmen, while a well-dressed boy stands in the doorway of the library.

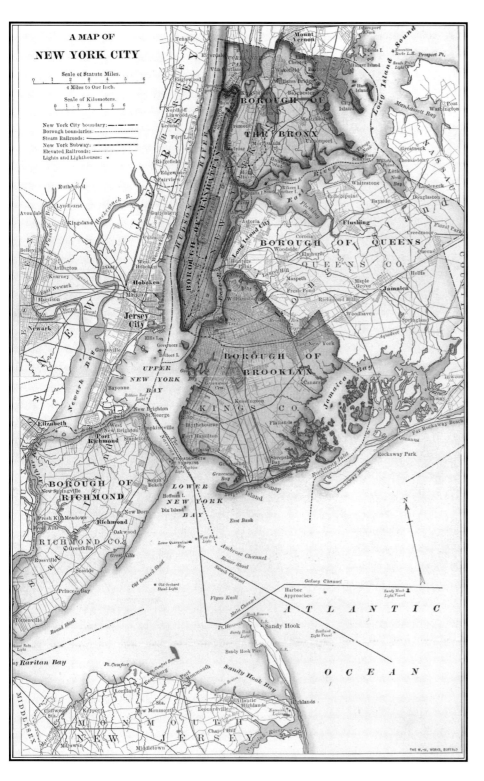

A MAP OF
NEW YORK CITY

The law establishing Greater New York went into effect on January 1, 1898. Queens County originally stretched east to Suffolk, but it was split when Long Island City, the towns of Newtown, Jamaica and Flushing, and part of Hempstead became one of the five boroughs; a year later the townships of Hempstead, North Hempstead and Oyster Bay formed Nassau County. With the consolidation of Queens into Greater New York, the Long Island City Library opened its branches to all residents of the new borough on February 28, 1898.

Right: A circulating library for adults opened in the Poppenhusen Institute in College Point in 1884, supported by private donations. Half the books and periodicals were in German.

Left: On January 1, 1901, four independent libraries were consolidated with the Queens Library: the Ozone Park Free Circulating Library; the Richmond Hill Free Library; the Hollis Public Library; and the Queens [Village] Free Library. The Ozone Park Branch moved to this rented storefront at 4138 Broadway on October 1, 1901, remaining there until 1923.

Below: The Williamsburg Bridge opened on December 19, 1903, after eight years of construction. At 1600-feet, it was the longest suspension span in the world, surpassing the far more graceful Brooklyn Bridge by five feet. This quickened development of Ridgewood and Middle Village.

Below, left and right:
As the Borough of Queens grew in the early decades of the century, there was enormous investment in essential urban infrastructure, particularly sewers and water mains, streets and sidewalks, gas and electricity. The Brooklyn Union Gas workmen pictured here are posing on new gas stoves and meters in about 1910. The two uniformed men provided service to private customers in homes or apartments, ca. 1915. Sponsored by Brooklyn Union.

On August 18, 1904, the Far Rockaway Branch opened. The first of the
Carnegie libraries in Queens, this one-story brick, limestone and terra-cotta
building burned in 1962. Sponsored by Forte Food Service Inc.

Girls practicing needlepoint while one of them reads aloud in the
Carnegie library in College Point, Poppenhusen Branch, 1912.

Above: The Carnegie library in Astoria opened on November 19, 1904. Dr. John S. Billings, director of the New York Public Library, was the featured speaker for the occasion. Here children pose in front of the building, ca. 1910.

Left: Children's room, Richmond Hill Branch, 1910.

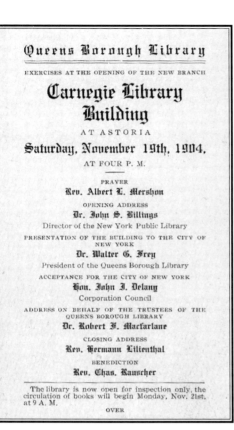

MAIN FLOOR PLAN, RICHMOND HILL BRANCH.

Above: The Library-School Garden Club, Poppenhusen Branch, 1915.
The Carnegie library in College Point opened on October 5, 1904. The
firm of Heins & La Farge, whose other credits included the original IRT
subway stations, the Bronx Zoo and the Cathedral of St. John the
Divine, designed the structure.

Left: The Carnegie library in Richmond Hill opened for public
inspection on Sunday, July 2, 1905. William Man and Alrick H. Man,
developers of Richmond Hill and Kew Gardens, had sold the site to
the city for $12,000; the total cost was $44,659.20.

Right: Mary Ann Shaw, the former principal of the Colored School in Flushing and wife of John W. A. Shaw, minister of the African Methodist Episcopal Church, died in 1905. She bequeathed $1,000 to the Flushing Free Library. Since no institution by that name existed, the ensuing legal tangle resolved her bequest as establishing the Shaw Reference Collection in the Flushing Branch, where her photograph hung for many years. She also left $40,000 to the Tuskeegee Institute.

Below: The Bayside Branch on Bell Boulevard opened on June 4, 1906, with Margaret J. Solon as librarian.

The Carnegie library in Elmhurst opened on March 31, 1906. The total cost for the site, building, books and equipment was $46,246.75. The architects were Lord & Hewlett, who also designed the Flushing and Far Rockaway branches. Elizabeth V. Dobbins was the librarian in charge. Sponsored by Cord Meyer Development Company.

62

Children looking through stereopticons, Elmhurst Branch, ca. 1915.
Sponsored by Cord Meyer Development Company.

Above: Children reading in the Broadway Branch, 1910. Notice the coal stove in the corner and the reproduction of the famous painting of "Washington Crossing the Delaware" on the wall.

Right: Jessie Hume (center) was named Chief Librarian on December 13, 1907; she had joined the Long Island City Public Library when it was formed in 1896 and served until 1919.

Facing page: The Broadway Branch, located at 491 Broadway in Long Island City, opened on June 20, 1906. Agnes R. Gillette was the librarian in charge. Sponsored by Quinn & Stamatiades, Funeral Directors.

On May 1, 1907, the library of the Social League of Whitestone, with fewer than 900 volumes in "a very small and uncomfortable room," was consolidated with the Queens Library and renamed the Whitestone Branch (the League had formed their private library for members the year before). The Branch moved into this wood-frame building in February 1908. Sponsored by Time Warner Cable of New York City.

Above: The Library's Department of Children's Work was created on January 2, 1908, under Harriot Hassler. This 1913 photograph shows the Boys History Club in the Nelson Branch. Sponsored by Davidoff & Malito.

Below: Librarian and children in the Whitestone Branch, 1910.

The Queensboro Bridge under construction, 1908.

Middle left:
The offices of the
Consolidated
Edison Company
in Bridge Plaza,
ca. 1912.

Middle right:
Queens grew rapidly
after the opening of
the Queensboro
Bridge, requiring
municipal services
and utilities.
Pictured here is
Astoria generating
station, 1908.

Right: The Con
Edison fleet, 1914.
All photographs
this page sponsored
by Consolidated
Edison of New York,
Queens Customer
Service.

After eight years of construction, the Queensboro Bridge opened to traffic on March 30, 1909. Here a parade of citizens and dignitaries prepares to march across from Manhattan during the official dedication in June. Sponsored by Consolidated Edison of New York, Queens Customer Service.

A deposit collection opened in a drugstore in Springfield on July 6, 1909, relocating to the Springfield Development Office (pictured here) the next year. Sponsored by NYNEX.

Above: The Woodside Station was designated a branch on June 19, 1910.
The neighborhood had been served by a traveling station since July 1908.

Left: The Mothers' Milk Station in Astoria, 1912. Mothers brought their infants to the city's milk station, where they received free milk and a checkup from a doctor. The Library put up a poster with a picture of the Astoria Branch and a list of "Books for Better Babies."

Above: The Middle Village Station, established in this candy store in September 1911. Here children wait their turn to enter. Sponsored by Home Federal Savings Bank.

Below: Librarian charging out books in the Middle Village Station, 1911.

A traveling library station was set up in Emener's Real Estate in the Evergreen section (pictured here) on July 20, 1910. That year other stations were established in Winfield in Zrubeck's Drug Store on Woodside Avenue, and in Woodhaven, Ridgewood and Corona.

The Corona Station moved into this rented storefront at 13 Locust Street (43rd Avenue) and was designated a branch on May 27, 1911. Sponsored by GreenPoint Bank.

Kelly's Picture Store, location of the Corona Station, September 1910. Sponsored by GreenPoint Bank.

Above: A traveling station was set up in this drug store in Rockaway Park in June 1911. The library was just the small table in the center (notice the attached stools which swing out). Other stations were opened that year in Glendale, Maspeth and Union Course. The Broadway Station, ancestor of the McGoldrick Branch, opened in the Rickert-Finlay Realty Company in Flushing. Sponsored by DeMatteis Construction Corp.

Facing page: The administrative offices of the Library were relocated from Long Island City to Colonial Hall in Jamaica on May 1, 1911. Also home of the Jamaica Branch, the antebellum structure was originally a private girls' school and then a boarding house. Left: Librarians pose on the lawn, 1913. Sponsored by Havens & Lombard, Esqs.

Above: Story hours for children were begun at each branch in 1911. This photograph of the Astoria Branch was part of the city's exhibit at the Pan American Exposition in San Francisco in 1914, celebrating the opening of the Panama Canal. Photographs this page sponsored by Korea News Inc.

Left: Men of the United States Life Saving Service in the Rockaways with books provided by the Queens Library, September 1911. There were life saving stations along the entire length of Long Island's Atlantic shore, with men ready to row out through the surf to aid ships in distress.

Above: The Traveling Library Department distributed books to 34 firehouses in 1911. Seen here are the men of Hose Company No. 4 in Jamaica.

Above: The Traveling Library Department sent books to each of the borough's 11 police precincts in early 1913.

Above: Off-duty railroad men using the library station in the YMCA at the Long Island Rail Road's Jamaica Station, 1912. By company rule they had to be out of uniform. Within the next few years, the Library distributed books to Sunday schools, Flushing Hospital, the Fort Totten army post and other sites.

Right: Library exhibit, complete with model airplanes, installed in City Hall to convince the City to increase the institution's budget, 1911. Harriot Hassler, head of the children's section, reported to head librarian Jessie Hume that "aeroplane fever is still raging among the boys." At Woodside "one boy was found copying the text—page-by-page—from certain chapters in Collins' Boys' book of model aeroplanes because he said, 'I can't keep this book longer than two weeks, and I can't make more than one aeroplane in that time,'" adding that he had waited a long time for his turn with the book.

Below: Interior of a Queens movie house, showing the Library's lantern slide superimposed on the screen, 1912. To increase circulation, the Library initiated new outreach measures. Lantern slides depicting the local branch, children's story hour and suggestions for reading were sent to movie houses. Typical slides included: "There are Polish books at the Public Library. Free to All" and "The Public Library is the working man's college. Use it." Sponsored by Keystone Electronics Corp.

Story hour at the Seaside Branch in the Rockaways, 1913. The Children's Department reported that children used the library in summer when it was too hot to play outside, "and nearly all Branches have had very full reading rooms on bitter cold days when the Library is one of the few comfortable places accessible." The report also singled out the use of the branches by 12- to 14-year olds "because they've no place else that is equally wholesome to go," adding that it would be a real loss to the community if the library were closed in the evenings. Sponsored by Eagle InterCommunications, Inc.

The Cedar Manor Station was located in this candy store from 1913 to 1923.

A station was established at the Parental School on May 29, 1913 (now Jefferson Hall on the Queens College campus). Sponsored by Citibank.

Above: Stations were established in PS 83 in Ravenswood and PS 76 in Laurel Hill (pictured here) in 1914. This was before schools had libraries of their own. Photographs this page sponsored by Jackson, Lewis, Schnitzler and Krupman, PC and Anthony and Clifford Atlas, Esqs.

Left: The Library opened stations for prisoners, both men and women, in the Queens County Jail in Hunters Point on September 10, 1915, offering a collection of about 800 volumes. Circulation topped 5,000 by the end of the year.

In 1921, the St. Albans station, originally set up in 1918, was moved to this former lunch wagon parked in a vacant lot, where it stayed for five years. The Mothers' Club had purchased the wagon for $300.

Below: Exposing children to great art was one of the earliest goals of the Children's Department. Here, boys study beneath reproductions of works by Raphael, 1912.

Above: President Woodrow Wilson addressed a joint session of Congress on April 2, 1917 to request a formal declaration of war against Germany, bringing the United States into the First World War. The libraries offered facilities for Liberty Loan drives and the Red Cross, sponsored book drives for soldiers and raised funds to buy reading matter for servicemen. Twenty-two hundred people filled the Jamaica Theatre on Wednesday, October 17, 1917 and raised $1,100 for the National Library Fund to buy books for military camps.

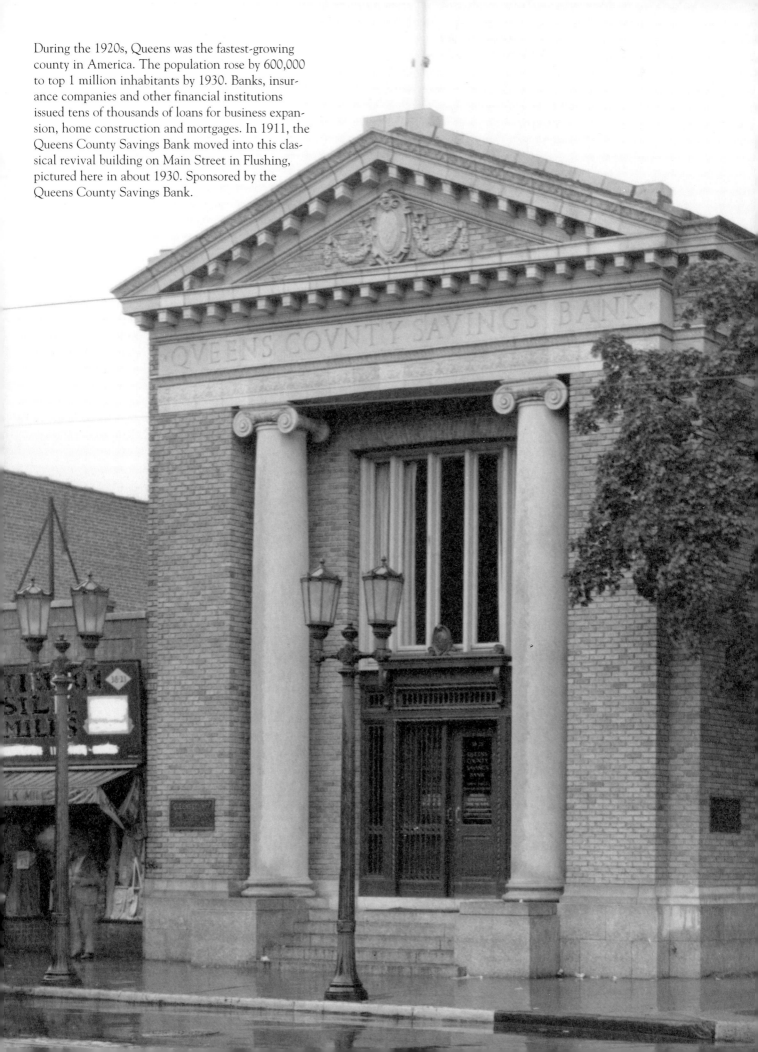

During the 1920s, Queens was the fastest-growing county in America. The population rose by 600,000 to top 1 million inhabitants by 1930. Banks, insurance companies and other financial institutions issued tens of thousands of loans for business expansion, home construction and mortgages. In 1911, the Queens County Savings Bank moved into this classical revival building on Main Street in Flushing, pictured here in about 1930. Sponsored by the Queens County Savings Bank.

The Woodhaven Branch opened to the public on January 7, 1924, in a new
building at 85-41 Forest Parkway, built with city funds and the last of the
Carnegie money. Within a month, librarians reported there were only 11
children's books left on the shelves. Sponsored by Congdon, Flaherty,
O'Callaghan, Reid, Donlon, Travis & Fishlinger.

The Elmhurst Manor (pictured here) and Blissville Stations opened in 1924.
Sponsored by Wright Risk Management.

The Library established its own library school on October 3, 1927. Four classes graduated by 1931, but the school was closed because the American Library Association refused to accredit any program not affiliated with a degree-granting institution. These women were the first graduates, 1928. Sponsored by the Queens County Savings Bank.

As the borough's population grew during the Roaring Twenties, older communities matured and new neighborhoods were built. Here, Martin A. Gleason (on the steps) supervises a funeral in Flushing, where he established his business in 1913. Sponsored by Martin A. Gleason, Inc., Funeral Home.

The 1906 Carnegie library in Flushing, shown here in about 1930. Sponsored by Martin A. Gleason, Inc., Funeral Home.

Above: The Ridgewood Branch opened at 20-12 Madison Street on October 15, 1929. Except for the Central Library in Jamaica and the Carnegie library in Woodhaven, this was the only branch building constructed in Queens during the boom years of the 1920s, and the first built entirely with municipal funds.

Left: The main branch of the Ridgewood Savings Bank (established in 1921) at Forest and Myrtle Avenues, opened in 1930. This photograph dates from the early 1950s, based on the presence of parking meters, which first appeared on curbs in 1951. Photographs this page sponsored by the Ridgewood Savings Bank.

Jo Carroll was appointed the system's official storyteller in 1929. She traveled to all of the branches and visited schools and community groups; every Thursday afternoon she broadcast stories over radio station WWRL. "Good stories still appeal to children in spite of the movies and the tabloids," she asserted. Here she visits the Woodside Branch, 1929. Sponsored by Eagle InterCommunications Inc.

On November 1, 1929, Mayor Jimmy Walker dedicated the Central Library. Carved in stone above the front door were the words, "These hoards of wealth you can unlock at will" (William Wordsworth, "The Excursion," Book IV). Designed by R.F. Schirmer and J.W. Schmidt, the Renaissance-revival, four-story structure opened on April 1, 1930. With construction of the current building in 1966, the Parsons Boulevard building became the Family Court.

The *Pioneer*, the original book bus, made its debut in 1930, bringing library materials to the outlying neighborhoods of the borough and those places which had grown quickly but did not have a nearby branch. It was christened by Mayor Walker on April 11 with a bottle containing water (it was during Prohibition, after all!) from Jamaica, Flushing and Little Neck Bays, the East River and the Atlantic Ocean, the bodies of water which bordered Queens. Marie Kohler, daughter of municipal budget director Charles L. Kohler, had the honor of breaking the bottle. With a capacity of 2,000 volumes, the bus also carried artistic and historical pictures, mainly for teachers (2,500 circulated in 1933). Fitted with a radio and loudspeaker, it broadcast children's stories read over municipal radio station WNYC.

Dedication of the *Pioneer* in front of City Hall, 1930.

The book bus began serving Baisley Park and Ravenswood on July 17, 1930 and Queens Plaza and Queensboro Hill the next day. Here a librarian sits at the charging desk, just behind the driver's seat.

The *Pioneer* making a regularly scheduled stop at the terminus of the elevated line on Liberty Avenue, 1930. Sponsored by Previte Farber & Rosen P.C.

In October, the *Pioneer* traveled to Albany for the New York Library Association conference and called on Governor Franklin Delano Roosevelt. He inspected the vehicle and received a library card, which he renewed annually.

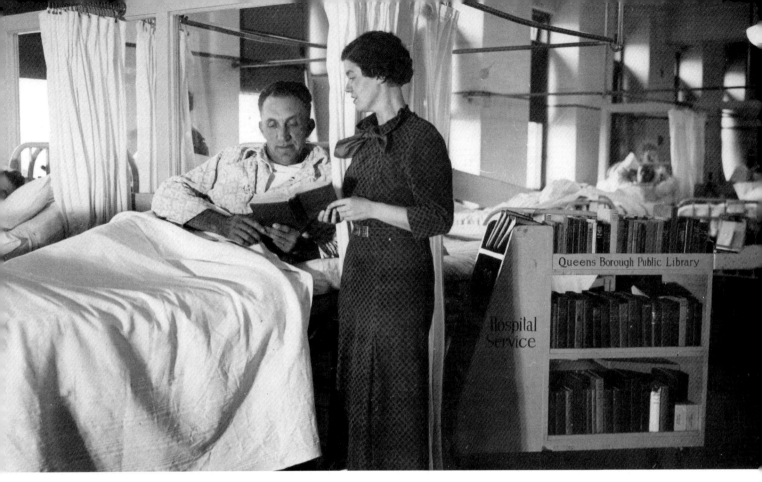

Above: A librarian was appointed for hospital work in 1932. By 1940, there was a new service for shut-ins and library work in seven hospitals, including Flushing Hospital, the Convalescent Home for Hebrew Children in Rockaway Park and the Hospital for Joint Diseases in Far Rockaway. Here a librarian makes the rounds in Queens General Hospital, 1936. Sponsored by Minolta Business Systems.

Below: Young readers in the Convalescent Home for Hebrew Children in Rockaway Park, ca. 1935.

This photograph of the entire staff of the Queens Borough Public Library was taken on the steps of the Central Library on June 11, 1933. In the front row, center, are Bess Fay Shipley, president of the Staff Association; George W. Pople, president of the Board of Trustees; Charles S. Colden, Queens District Attorney; and Owen S. Dever, library director.

Above: A crowd of 500 witnessed the cornerstone laying ceremony for the new Glendale Branch to be constructed by the WPA [Works Progress Administration], 1935. A copper box set in the cornerstone contained a list of Library trustees, local newspapers, three lead plates telling the history of the building project, and coins and name cards tossed in by spectators.

Above: The Glendale Branch opened to the public in a new building at 78-60 73rd Place at Myrtle Avenue on January 2, 1937. The Renaissance Revival structure, erected with WPA funds and labor, featured medallions representing great writers: Swift, Shakespeare, Longfellow, Burns, Voltaire, Homer, Dante and Goethe.

Right: Work on the new addition to the Astoria Branch began on August 17, 1936, a WPA project that provided employment for 50 men. WPA artist Max Spivak's new murals, "Circus Puppets," graced the children's room.

Below: The WPA mural "The Story of Richmond Hill" was completed in the Richmond Hill Branch in 1936. The artistic style caused some controversy at the time. "Maybe we are small town folks," one resident remarked, "but it strikes us that parts of the body are too accentuated."

The Library's report on the occasion of its 40th anniversary in 1936 noted: "If it had not been for the assistance of the WPA clerks and librarians assigned to the Library, many of its services would necessarily have been cut short. With their help all essential activities have been maintained, and through the securing of many workers trained in special fields much additional work has been accomplished which would not otherwise have been possible."

The *Pioneer* was retired in February 1938 due to its dilapidated condition. A car continued the route until a new bus began running a year later.

The Woodside Branch opened in its new brick building at 54-22 Skillman Avenue on January 9, 1937. Completed in 1933, it had remained empty. Buk Ulrich created murals showing the history of writing for the children's room, and "The Acquisition of Long Island" by James D. Brooks (pictured here) looked down on the main reading room. The murals were lost during later renovations.

The new children's room in the expanded Ridgewood Branch, 1937.
Photographs this page sponsored by Bisys, Inc.

In 1937, expansion of the Ridgewood
Branch was completed after two years of
work. WPA funds had made possible two
new wings and an added balcony.

Municipal radio station WNYC discontinued its broadcasts of the Queens Library's "Story Hour" in 1938. The Library's annual report called that "our greatest sorrow this year." Sponsored by Kekst and Company.

Interior of the second book bus, *Progress*, June 22, 1939.

In a brief ceremony at City Hall on March 2, 1939, Mayor La Guardia christened the new book bus, *Progress.* He applied for the first card, listing his occupation as "civic worker." The new vehicle cost about $7,500. Its first stop the following Monday was PS 2, 21st Avenue and 75th Street in North Woodside, then PS 147 in St. Albans, PS 162 in Bayside, and the intersection of 58th Avenue and Main Street in Flushing. These children are waiting their turn to enter. Sponsored by 89th Jamaica Realty Co.

The Art and Music Division
acquired phonograph records
they made available for listen-
ing in the library using an
Ansley Dynaphone radio
phonograph equipped with
dual headphones. Records
began circulating in 1947.
Sponsored by Information
Access Company.

The New York World's Fair opened on April 30, 1939. President Roosevelt's opening address was the first presidential speech to be televised. Only a few technicians saw the broadcast, however. Flushing Meadow had been the City's largest garbage dump before it was transformed into "The World of Tomorrow." The Fair ran for two seasons and included pavilions by many corporations and foreign countries. These postcards (below and right) show the Fair's symbol, the Trylon and Perisphere and the American Telephone and Telegraph pavilion.

The Queensboro Hill Station was established on November 25, 1940. The WPA funded the remodeling of a building erected for the World's Fair.

Left: The Forest Hills Branch, forced out of its home in August, reopened on November 3, 1946, in a "temporary" building at 108-19 71st Avenue, erected through public subscription. A permanent home for the branch was not built for another decade. Sponsored by Councilman Morton Povman, 24th District, Queens.

Below: In honor of the institution's golden anniversary, Borough President James A. Burke declared October 30, 1946, "Queens Borough Public Library Day." The Sanitation Department Band provided entertainment for the ceremony in front of the Central Library. Sponsored by EBSCO Subscription Services.

The Library celebrated its 50th Anniversary in 1946 with a gala dinner at the Hotel Commodore on November 14, 1946. Five hundred guests attended the affair (at $5 per person) which featured operatic works by the lyric soprano Ethel Barrymore Colt and an address by author Christopher Morley. Morley presented a collection of 15 letters by William Cullen Bryant to the Library. The proceedings were broadcast live over municipal radio station WNYC. Sponsored by Chase Manhattan Bank.

Fiftieth
ANNIVERSARY
Dinner

1896 - 1946

THE QUEENS BOROUGH PUBLIC LIBRARY

Right: Children in front of the Pomonok Branch, 1962.

Below left: On August 1, 1951, the McGoldrick Branch moved into a new building rented under a long-term lease at 162-15 Depot Road. The children's room was up the small flight of stairs.

Branches were established in four public housing projects. The Pomonok Branch opened on June 17, 1951. The Arverne Branch opened in June in the Arverne Houses. A branch opened in the Woodside Houses in June, but it closed in 1958. In July, the Ravenswood Branch (seen here) opened in the Ravenswood Houses.

Ground breaking for the Steinway Branch, 1954. Chief Librarian Harold W. Tucker is on the left. Photographs this page sponsored by Steinway & Sons.

The Steinway Branch was dedicated on May 21, 1956. Construction had begun on October 5, 1954, and the total cost was $308,000. A pre-school room and parents' lounge were upstairs. Note the picture of William Steinway, the same one which hung in the first Steinway library in 1890.

Ground breaking for the Jackson Heights Branch, 1952.

The Jackson Heights Branch at 35-51 81st Street opened on October 26, 1954. Sponsored by Meridian Capital Funding, Inc.

The Queens Village Branch, located at 94-11 217th Street, opened on June 8, 1952. The site had been purchased in 1937 for $30,000. Design was approved in 1948, and the ground breaking was in 1950; the final cost, including furnishings, books and property was $400,000. Architect Raymond Irrera of Long Island City won an award from the Queensborough Chamber of Commerce for the design. In 1956, the branch opened a total of 65 hours a week.

Above: The new Flushing Library, which replaced the 1906 Carnegie library, was dedicated on June 18, 1957, the third library building on the site. Sponsored by Koryo Book Importing, Inc.

Below: The ground-breaking ceremony for the Broadway Branch at 40-20 Broadway in Astoria, April 18, 1956. The building was dedicated on October 29, 1957. Sponsored by Connie and George L. Stamatiades.

The new Fresh Meadows Branch at 193-20 Horace Harding Expressway was dedicated on September 22, 1958, and opened to the public the next day. This is the architect's rendering (below) and a plan for furnishing the main floor (right).

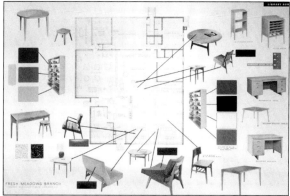

The second World's Fair opened in Flushing Meadows on the site of the 1939 World's Fair. The Unisphere represented the Fair's theme, "Peace Through Understanding." Queens Library Director Harold W. Tucker was Chairman of the American Library Association's World's Fair Committee, and was primarily responsible for the popular LIBRARY U.S.A. exhibit. Pictured on the facing page are visitors to the fair in April 1964, with the Unisphere in the background. The Bell Systems pavilion at the World's Fair included a 15-minute ride through the history of communications and exhibits of contemporary technology. Sponsored by AT&T.

Right: Crowded conditions in the adult reading room in the Central Library on Parsons Boulevard, December 1963. Sponsored by Queensborough Community College/CUNY.

Below: The Howard Beach Branch, the 52nd in the system, opened on April 27, 1963. Here, a Cub Scout delivers a flyer announcing the opening.

Below: Operation Headstart story hour, Queensbridge Branch, March 11, 1965. The program introduced pre-schoolers to books, and included special training for parents and programs for teens. It predated the Federal Head Start program by six months.

The Central Library moved into its new home at 89-11 Merrick Boulevard in Jamaica, leaving its elegant but cramped home of 36 years on Parsons Boulevard, on March 21, 1966. The new building opened on April 11. This was the first major branch of an urban library where all public services were on one floor (195,000 square feet). The total cost was $5,703,971; the architects were York & Sawyer, Kiff, Colean, Voss & Souder. The first person to sign for a card in the new building was 88-year old Michael Ettlinger.

Below: Headstart story hour, 1965. The librarian blew out the candle at the end of the session.

119

Above: The North Hills Branch opened in a rented store-front at 245-06 Horace Harding Expressway in 1964. This is the staff on opening day, with an admirer. Sponsored by The Roslyn Savings Bank.

The Library created the "Library-Go-Round" bus to bring books to small children in 1967, later adding the "Tell-a-Tale Trailer" for older children and the "Library in Action Teenmobile."

Song session in the Library-Go-Round, 1967. Sponsored by R.Y. Management Co., Inc.

Right: In March 1969, the city's budget director requested that the Queens Library submit a plan to implement a cut of more than 20%. A public outcry mitigated the cuts from the originally proposed $1.7 million to "only" $300,000. At the North Hills Branch (pictured here), children staged a demonstration out front, carrying protest signs which read "We got a snow job in February, don't book us now" and "Last on the list for snow removal...First on the list for library removal" and "An Investment in knowledge pays the best dividend," Benjamin Franklin.

Below: Architect's rendering, Vleigh Branch, 1963. Typical of the modern buildings erected in the 1960s, the Vleigh Branch was dedicated in March 1967.

Top: The Langston Hughes Community Library and Cultural Center at 102-09 Northern Boulevard opened on April 7, 1969, in a former toy warehouse (originally a Woolworth's). Sponsored by Astoria Federal Savings.

Below: The After School Reading Program began at the Laurelton and Baisley Park Branches in 1982; the next year it was extended to Arverne. The areas selected were characterized by low reading scores for elementary school children. The program provided remedial tutoring in reading and writing for 12-year-olds, serving up to 30 children at each branch. There were also workshops for parents.

Above: A fire destroyed the Rego Park Branch on February 20, 1972. The neighborhood relied on the bookmobile until the new building opened in 1975.

Below: The Rego Park Branch, mid-1950s.

Above: A fire in the Woodhaven Branch on June 17, 1978 forced its closing until June 2, 1980. Two teenagers were accused of the crime, leading to cries for a curfew in the neighborhood.

Right: Children demonstrating in front of the Bellerose Branch, March 1977.

Right: Opening day at the new Bellerose Branch, February 27, 1978; the branch had been completed almost a year earlier, but the fiscal crisis postponed the opening.

Right: Computerized check-out was initiated at the Lefferts Reference Center in 1978. In succeeding months, other branches closed for a few days to put bar codes in all the books.

At a press conference on June 16, 1986, Director Constance B. Cooke announced the results of a Gallup survey commissioned by the Library which showed that over half the residents of Queens held library cards; 69% had charged out materials in the preceding year (averaging six items per person). Fewer than a third of the borough's Hispanic residents had cards, however. The Director announced additional funds for Spanish materials, increased efforts to recruit Spanish-speaking staff and volunteers and created the *Say Si,* collection to attract Hispanic users. Sponsored by the Bilingual Publications Company.

"Queens Quick Cat," a CD-ROM catalog of the system's entire holdings, was introduced in April 1988.

By 1995, collections in more than 40 languages were available at the Central Library's Literature and Languages Division and at branches throughout the system. *Say Si*, the Spanish-language collection, held 78,000 items in 20 branches; *Ni Hao*, 75,000 items in Chinese in 28 branches; *Hannara*, 15,000 items in Korean in 10 branches; and *Namaste-Adaab*, 8,000 items in South Asian languages at five branches.

The Francis Lewis High School marching Band in front of the Central Library on "Charter Day," March 19, 1996. The Library celebrated its first century of service with a host of festivities throughout the system. On that day Queens Library also unveiled its home page on the World Wide Web: http://www.queens.lib.ny.us

Mayor Rudolph Giuliani, Borough President Claire Shulman and Director Gary E. Strong viewing the Centennial exhibit in the Queens Library Gallery on the date of the Library's 100th anniversary—"Charter Day," March 19, 1996.

New York City Mayor Rudolph W. Giuliani (at the podium) addresses
a black-tie throng of Library supporters and other Queens dignitaries
at the Centennial Benefit Dinner Dance on September 21, 1996.
Proceeds from the event established the Queens Library Foundation's
"Futures Fund," an endowment for the purchase of library materials
for children.

Proceeds from the Library's Centennial Benefit Dinner Dance and from the sale of this book contributed start-up funding for the "Futures Fund"—an endowment to provide books and other library materials for the children of Queens.

On September 21, 1996, the Library held its Centennial Benefit Dinner Dance at Terrace on the Park. Built by the Port Authority of New York and New Jersey for the 1964 World's Fair, the unusual building featured a heliport on the roof. This photo dates from 1964; the General Motors pavilion from the Fair is visible in the background. Sponsored by Terrace on the Park.

Acknowledgments

This Centennial history of the Queens Library is the product of many dedicated people: Dr. Jeffrey A. Kroessler, who prepared the text and identified photos, and members of the Queens Library's Long Island Division, including Charles Young and William Asadorian, who reviewed the historical record which this volume commemorates.

Thanks also to those who worked on its production, and the myriad details which that involves: Queens Library Foundation staff members, including Stanley Gornish, Judith Poretz, Ray Nill, Renee Hassell, Joseph Simmons and Ronald Kastner; and the Library's Public Relations Department, including Frank Carollo, Jay Aberbach and Fran Saliani.

And of course, grateful recognition must be given to the many individuals who, currently and over the last century, have dedicated their working lives to enable the Queens Borough Public Library to "light the way" for the people of Queens.

We extend our appreciation to the individuals and institutions whose significant contributions to the Foundation have benefitted the Queens Borough Public Library's programs and services.

The following donors contributed to the establishment of *The Futures Fund* by sponsoring photos in this book, purchasing tickets for the Centennial Benefit Dinner Dance, or by providing other financial support.

Benefactors

AT&T
The Billy Rose Foundation, Inc.
Brooklyn Union
Chase Manhattan Bank
Citibank
Consolidated Edison of New York, Queens Customer Service
GreenPoint Bank
Information Access Company
NYNEX
Queens County Savings Bank
Ridgewood Savings Bank
Time Warner Cable of New York City

Patrons

The Bilingual Publications Company
Bisys, Inc.
Cord Meyer Development Company
Eagle InterCommunications Inc.
Havens & Lombard, Esqs.
Korea News Inc.
Martin A. Gleason, Inc., Funeral Home

Friends

Astoria Federal Savings
Koryo Book Importing, Inc.
Queensborough Community College/CUNY

Sponsors

89th Jamaica Realty Co.
Antun's Caterers of Queens Village
ARSI Foundation
ATCO Properties & Management, Inc.
Baker & Taylor
Ben's Kosher Deli & Restaurant Corp.
Beroff Associates
Book Wholesalers, Inc.
The Bookmen, Inc.
Brodart Co.
Brooklyn Public Library
Caffé On the Green
California Language Laboratories
Capital Cleaning Contractors, Inc.
Carl Bloom Associates, Inc.
Central Auto Inc.
Certified Glass Corp.
Charles Schmidgall & Associates Inc.
Columbian Civic Center
Community Mediation Services Inc.
Compact Disc World, Inc.
Congdon, Flaherty, O'Callaghan, Reid, Donlon, Travis & Fishlinger
Cooke Abstract Corp.
Cross County Federal Savings Bank
David Mammina, Architect
Davidoff & Malito
Davidson Titles, Inc.
DeMatteis Construction Corp.
Discovery Networks
EBSCO Subscription Services
First Baptist Church of East Elmhurst
Flushing Savings Bank
Forte Food Service Inc.
Frederick Services Inc. Funeral Home
Friends of Queen Catherine, Inc.
Gerald J. Caliendo, Architect
Gibney, Anthony & Flaherty, LLP
Graubard Mollen & Miller
Himalaya Foundation
Home Federal Savings Bank
Ideal Foreign Books Inc.
Isabella Geriatric Center, Inc.
Jackson, Lewis, Schnitzler & Krupman
Kalvin-Miller International, Inc.
Keefe, Bruyette & Woods, Inc.
Kekst and Company
Keystone Electronics Corp.

S. Klenosky, Inc.
LaGuardia Community College
Lakhi General Contractor Inc.
Latin American Cultural Center of Queens, Inc.
London Towncars, Inc.
Loomis Sayles & Company, L.P.
Lord & Taylor
Lord Burgess Music Pub. Co.
Lorilil Jewelers
Martin Neville & McIntyre Ltd.
Mattone, Mattone & Co.
Meridian Capital Funding, Inc.
Metropolitan Diagnostic Medical Lab
Midwest Library Service
Minolta Business Systems
Napoleon Cafe Restaurant
New York Hospital - Queens
Peck's Office Plus
Peninsula Hospital Center
Petracca & Sons, Inc.
Positive Promotions
Previte Farber & Rosen P.C.
Queens Council on the Arts
Queens Museum of Art
Queens News and Smoke Shop
Queens Theatre in the Park
Quinn & Stamatiades, Funeral Directors
R.Y. Management Co., Inc.
Retirement System Group Inc.
The Roslyn Savings Bank
Silberberg Associates, Inc.
Smith Automation Systems, Inc.
State Bank of Long Island
Steinway & Sons
Sterling & Sterling, Inc.
Sterling National Bank & Trust
Terrace on the Park
Theiss, Lipner & Co.
Tishman Construction Corporation of New York
Titleserv
Travers Tool Company, Inc.
W.J. Book Store, Inc.
Westbury Press, Inc.
World Journal
Wright Risk Management
United Cerebral Palsy - Queens
Unity Electric Co., Inc.

Sponsors

Thomas E. Alford

Vincent & Lois Arcuri

Darlene Askew

Joan Asselin

Joan Barnes

Louis Berger

Herbert Berman, Esq.

Dr. & Mrs. Canute Bernard

William Blake II

Frank L. Carollo

Rafael Castelar

Rosanne Cerny

James B. Chapin, Ph.D.

Julie Chase

Philip Click

Thomas E. Curley, Ph.D.

Michael J. Daly

Mr. & Mrs. Charles A. De Benedittis

Carolyn De Loatch

DeMatteis Family

Mr. & Mrs. George Dixon

Frank Dominianni

Daniel G. Donahue

Roy M. Faust

Patricia Flynn

Sue Fontaine

Henry E. Froebel

Kathleen M. Furlong

Thomas W. Galante

Joan M. Ganly

Dr. Rose M. Gil

Stanley E. Gornish

Mr. & Mrs. Paul Gibson

Denise Gray

Hon. Robert T. Groh

Herbert Grolnick

Mary Haines

Raymond Irrera & Associates

Andrew P. Jackson

William Jefferson

John P. Kane

G. Ronald Kastner, Ph.D.

Valerie Kilmartin

Sophie Kline

Frank Kotnik

Mark Lii

Marian S. Lubinsky

The Rev. Canon Dougald L. Maclean

Terri and Frank Mangino

Lois Marbach

Francis J. McKenna

Charles McMorran

Mr. & Mrs. Daniel Medina

Diane Metcalf

Josephine & Joel Miele

Nashralah Misk

Tallulah Noah

Dr. Winifred Latimer Norman

Nayibe Nuñez-Berger

Lucy C. Nunziato

Andrew Ohm

Marilyn Okrent

John Ottulich

Mr. & Mrs. William H. Owens

Lynn E. Owens

Linda Perno

Lorna Phillips

John A. Pileski

Councilman Morton Povman, 24th District Queens

Anita Rentrope

Mr. & Mrs. Rosemond A. Richardson, Sr.

Chariya Riengchandra

Arthur E. Rojas

Mr. & Mrs. Howard Rubenstein

Andrew N. Schlein, Ph.D.

Janet M. Schneider

Brenda & Elliot Semel

Carol L. Sheffer

Kenneth G. Sivulich

Christine & Archie Spigner

Connie & George L. Stamatiades

Edward M. Stein

Carolyn & Gary Strong

Sherman Tang, Ph.D.

Carmine Tedesco

Mr. & Mrs. Otis B. Turner

Marcia Voronovsky

Senator Alton R. Waldon, Jr.

Barbara Waldon

Robert J. Waters

and others whose contributions were received too late for inclusion.

Bibliographic Notes

All photographs and historical information in this book have been taken from the Long Island Division of the Queens Borough Public Library (except for certain photographs provided by the Queens County Savings Bank, Ridgewood Savings Bank, AT&T, Martin A. Gleason, Inc., Funeral Home, Consolidated Edison of New York, Brooklyn Union and Lord & Taylor). Information pertaining to the Queens Borough Public Library comes from the Library's internal reports, publications and documents, as well as from the files of the Long Island Division.

Suggested reading:

Jackson, Kenneth T., *The Encyclopedia of New York City*. New Haven: 1995.

Karatzas, Daniel, *Jackson Heights: A Garden in the City*. Jackson Heights: 1990.

Kroessler, Jeffrey A., *Building Queens: The Urbanization of New York's Largest Borough*. Unpublished thesis, CUNY Graduate School, 1991.

Kroessler, Jeffrey A., and Rappaport, Nina S., *Historic Preservation in Queens*. Queens: 1990.

Queens Borough Chamber of Commerce, *Queensborough Magazine*, 1913-date.

Seyfried, Vincent, and Asadorian, William, *Old Queens, N.Y., in Early Photographs*. New York: 1991.

Seyfried, Vincent, *Elmhurst: From Town Seat to Mega-Suburb*. Queens Community Series, 1995.

Seyfried, Vincent, *Queens, A Pictorial History*. Norfolk: 1982.

Seyfried, Vincent, *The Story of Corona*. Queens Community Series, 1986.

Seyfried, Vincent, *The Story of Queens Village*. Queens Community Series, 1974.

Seyfried, Vincent, *The Story of Woodhaven and Ozone Park*. Queens Community Series, 1985.

Seyfried, Vincent, *300 Years of Long Island City*. Queens Community Series, 1984.

Sherman, Franklin J., *Building Up Greater Queens Borough*. New York: 1929.

Willensky, Elliot, and White, Norval, *The AIA Guide to New York City*. New York: 1988.

Index

INDEX M
SECTION